INSIGHT POCKET GUIDE

Malta

D0306282

APA PUBLICATIONS
Part of the Langenscheidt Publishing Group

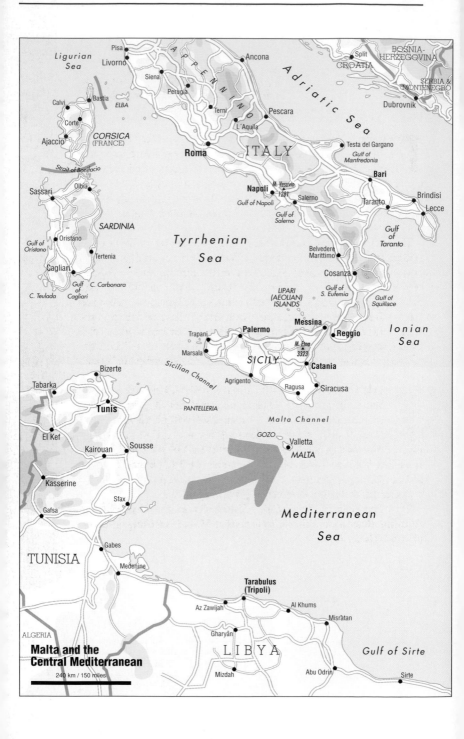

Malta and the
Central Mediterranean

240 km / 150 miles

Welcome

This is one of 133 itinerary-based Pocket Guides produced by the editors of Insight Guides, whose books have set the standard for visual travel guides since 1970. With top-quality photography and authoritative recommendations, this guidebook brings you the very best of Malta in a series of tailor-made routes devised by one of Insight's experts, Lyle Lawson, who has been visiting the islands of Malta and Gozo for many years, drawn by their unique culture and history.

The tours are designed to suit a range of time-frames and tastes. They include walking tours around Valletta, Mdina and Rabat, cities rich in Arab and Crusader history, several coastal hikes, drives into the interior, and two full-day options devoted to Malta's twin island of Gozo, just a 25-minute ferry ride away. There's also a selection of fun excursions, including an underwater safari with a glass-bottom boat, a cruise around the Maltese archipelago, fishing trips and Jeep tours. Supporting the itineraries are sections on history and culture, shopping, eating out, sports activities and festivals, as well as a fact-packed practical information section that includes a list of hand-picked hotels.

Lyle Lawson is a long-term devotee of Malta. Her work as a freelance writer and photographer takes her back time after time. She has scanned the terrain from a helicopter, descended to the depths of Ghar Hasan, hiked most of the southern coastline, won and lost money at the casino and has photographed more baroque churches on the islands than she can remember. In this book her main aim has been to show the diversity of Malta and the Maltese, a people whom she finds 'ebullient and very warm-hearted', characteristics that reflect their outgoing, seafaring history.

This edition of *Insight Pocket Guide: Malta* has been updated by **Geoffrey Aquilina Ross**, a journalist currently based in Malta and the original editor of *Insight Guide: Malta*.

GOZO'S HIGHLIGHTS

A full-day itinerary highlighting the main sights of Gozo, Malta's smaller neighbour, has been designed for visitors on a day-trip from Malta. For those with more time in Gozo, this is followed by two further options.

EXCURSIONS

A selection of fun excursions, including an underwater safari with a glass-bottom boat, a cruise around the Maltese archipelago, fishing trips and Jeep tours..........................**61**

LEISURE ACTIVITIES

Tips on shopping and sports activities and advice on the best places to eat **65–74**

CALENDAR OF EVENTS

A detailed list of Malta's main festivals **75**

PRACTICAL INFORMATION

All the background information you will need for your stay, including a discriminating list of hotels **77**

MAPS

INDEX AND CREDITS

pages **93–96**

Pages 2/3: Valletta and St Julian's from the air
Pages 8/9: messing about in a boat

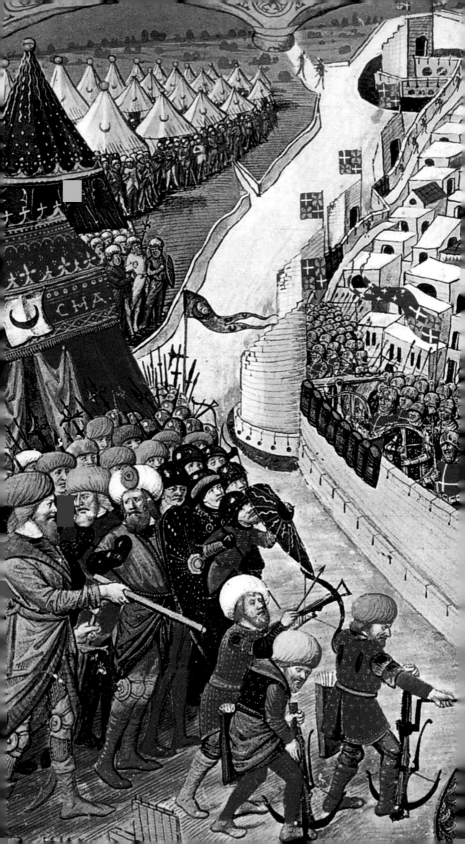

History & Culture

Malta's history has always been determined by its position in the middle of the Mediterranean. The island is 93km (58 miles) south of Sicily, and 352km (220 miles) north of Libya. Tunisia is 288km (180 miles) to the west and Lebanon is the nearest country to the east. Thus situated, it could not help but feature in the rise and fall of several civilisations.

The temples of Hagar Qim and Mnajdra on Malta and Ggantija on its sister island, Gozo, bear witness to a flourishing early Bronze Age (circa 3500 BC) civilisation. The Hypogeum, a subterranean burial place at Malta's Hal Saflieni, was carved into rocks over a period of hundreds of years between 2500 BC and 2000 BC with simple flint or obsidian tools. As the Greeks, Carthaginians and Romans established their empires, Malta became caught up in a series of Mediterranean conflicts.

During the Third Punic War, Malta's Grand Harbour became a Carthaginian naval base; when Carthage lost the war, the island was given to the Romans, who generally neglected it. In about AD 60, a ship that was taking St Paul to Rome, where he was due to stand trial, ran aground off Malta's northwestern coast. Indeed, Paul has been credited with laying the foundations of Christianity in Malta. Publius, the island's Roman governor, was an early convert, and by the 3rd century most islanders were Christians.

After the fall of Rome, Malta experienced a period of relative peace. Arabs conquered the island in 870 and ruled benignly. Their major legacy was linguistic: Arabic forms the basis for much of the Maltese language.

The Knights of St John

Count Roger the Norman, who was based in Sicily, conquered Malta in 1091, and for several hundred years the ruler of Sicily also ruled Malta. Although Ferdinand and Isabella, Spain's 'Catholic monarchs', won control of the island in the 15th century, it was not until 1565, when the Knights of St John of Jerusalem (or Knights Hospitallers) defeated the Arabs that Malta was confirmed as a Christian country. Founded in 1085, the order's original purpose was to care for pilgrims who fell ill on visits to the Holy Land. But when Godfrey de Bouillon, a leader of the first Crusade, captured Jerusalem in 1099 their role began to change. By the time the order was placed under papal protection in 1113, the Knights had become fighters, although they still protected and treated pilgrims.

After Jerusalem fell to Islam in 1187, Richard the Lionheart moved the order to Acre; when Sultan Kahil took that city in 1291, the Knights moved to Cyprus. Rhodes became the order's new home in 1310, and for over 200 years they fought, and beat, the Turks in the eastern Mediterranean. The Knights were unbeatable, their fortress island impregnable. But such invincibility

Left: siege of the Christian garrison
Right: Venus of Malta

could not last. In 1522 the Turks' Suleiman the Magnificent successfully attacked Rhodes. Six months later, he allowed the Knights to leave with their honour intact, but once again they were homeless.

In 1529 Charles V, the grandson of Ferdinand and Isabella, offered them residence in Malta, where they made Birgu (later named Vittoriosa) their base. The Maltese people were not party to the invitation but they welcomed the Knights as defenders against the Barbary Coast corsairs who were given to raiding and looting Malta and Gozo, taking slaves and hostages. In 1565 an Ottoman fleet of 181 ships, with more than 30,000 men, sailed from Constantinople with the intention of redeeming the Mediterranean for Allah. On 18 May the Turkish ships launched an attack on Fort St Elmo. The Knights were targeted by 7,000 rounds of ammunition every day, and on 23 June the Turks raised their flag over the fort. Fewer than a dozen Maltese survived, but the Turks also suffered heavy losses. They breached the walls of Birgu but the Knights resisted. When word arrived of reinforcements from Sicily the Turks retreated in ignominy. Once again the Knights' cross flew over the bastions of St Elmo.

The Saviour of Christendom

The Knights' leader, Grand Master Jean Parisot de la Valette, was declared the saviour of Christendom, and Birgu and Senglea were renamed Vittoriosa and Invicta. But the price was high: 220 Knights dead, 9,000 soldiers killed, countless wounded and the island's fortifications shattered. La Valette decided that a new capital was needed, and Mount Sceberras, near Fort St Elmo, was chosen. Designed by Francesco Laparelli, an aide to Michelangelo, Valletta, named after the Knights' leader, was inaugurated in 1566.

Two years later the Maltese architect and engineer, Gerolamo Cassar, was put in charge of building the city, and it is his work that we see today. One of his major projects included accommodation for the Knights' Eight Langues, or languages, representing Germany, Italy, Castile, Aragon, Provence, Auvergne, France and England. Having defeated the Turks, the Knights began to forget their vows of poverty, chastity and humility. The simple taverns of Vittoriosa were replaced by larger, more elaborate affairs, rich food and fine wines were consumed, elegant silk and brocade robes took the place of chain mail, and mistresses were openly flaunted. Worse still was the return of piracy, victimising not the Turks but fellow Christians.

When revolution erupted in France in 1789, many of the French Knights joined the Royalists or contributed money to Louis XVI. In 1791 they were deprived of their nationality and a year later the order's estates and revenues in France were confiscated. Deprived of their French revenues, the Knights looked for another source of income. The Russian Tsar Paul I offered to found an Orthodox Langue and assume the title of Protector of the Order. But the British, whose strategy was to keep both the Russians and the French out of the Mediterranean, initiated their own talks with Grand Master de Rohan-Polduc. Unfortunately, he died in 1797, before the negotiations could be completed.

The new Grand Master, Ferdinand de Hompesch, accepted the Russian offer. This enraged Napoleon to the extent that he left Italy – which he had just conquered – and dropped anchor outside the Grand Harbour in June 1798. When he was refused entry, he opened fire. After two days of shelling, the French landed and gave the Knights four days in which to pack their belongings and leave, thus ending their 268-year presence on Malta.

Nobody was sorry to see them go. The Maltese rejoiced and lit bonfires, the French soldiers looted their taverns and palaces and Napoleon had their hospital's silver service melted down to pay for his troops' expenses in Egypt before sailing off to fight elsewhere.

Capitulation of the French

After Napoleon's departure, the French troops became even more ruthless. The Maltese eventually responded by attacking the French garrison at Mdina. The French commander retreated to Valletta, and waited in vain for help from Napoleon. The locals blockaded Valletta's land approaches and a Portuguese fleet, later aided by a British squadron, protected the harbour against the return of Napoleon. The French force finally capitulated in 1800.

Sovereignty of the islands passed to Britain which, to the people of Malta, was preferable to the presence of either the French or the Knights. In 1814 Russia, no longer allied with France, formally renounced any intention of helping the Knights regain their position in Malta. The islands became a British crown colony and one of the empire's most loyal possessions. The

Left: Palace of the Knights fresco. **Top:** Grand Master Jean Parisot de la Valette
Right: invasion of the French, 1798

Maltese adopted the English language and law, and the island established itself as an important stop on the trade route from Britain to India. In World War I more than 25,000 allied casualties were treated in Malta.

The first self-governing constitution was granted in 1921. This left Britain in control of immigration and foreign policy and the Maltese responsible for domestic affairs. The 1930s saw a series of disagreements between the British governor general, the Church and local politicians. These internal conflicts were resolved by 1936, at a time when the whole continent was, to a greater or lesser degree, preparing for the great conflict to come.

Not surprisingly, given his militaristic ventures in Africa, and the island's proximity to Italy, Mussolini had designs on Malta. On 10 June 1940, he declared war against the Allies. The following day bombs started falling on Malta. At the time there were 30,000 British and Maltese troops on the island and a civilian population of around 250,000. The dry docks were among the most modern in Europe, which made the island particularly attractive to potential invaders. There was no shortage of politicians in London advocating the evacuation of Malta, and its submission to Il Duce, but Churchill was convinced of Malta's long-term strategic importance, and his view prevailed. The islands

defended themselves, and the people spent much of their time in air-raid shelters as Italian warplanes dropped their bombs day and night.

In 1941, with Mussolini's air force no closer to capturing Malta despite its overwhelming air supremacy, the German Luftwaffe entered the battle. The Nazis had one priority: to cut the island's supply lines. Without engine fuel, spare parts, oil and food, the islanders would have no choice but to surrender. The island did enjoy a brief respite when Germany's Field Marshal Rommel decided to concentrate on Tobruk, but the Nazis realised that they could not secure North Africa unless Malta was neutralised. As far as they were concerned, if Malta would not surrender, it could starve.

The Second Siege

The second great siege suffered by the island began in January 1942 and continued until April. Twice as many bombs fell on Malta as fell on London in a whole year at the height of the Blitz. Some 40,000 homes were destroyed and the islands were completely blockaded. In April George VI awarded the islands the George Cross. The citation reads: 'To honour a brave people I award the George Cross to the island fortress of Malta to bear witness to a heroism and a devotion that will long be famous in history.'

By mid-May Malta's situation had become desperate. The islanders had less than three months' supply of food, and if help did not arrive soon, they would have no option but to surrender. Fortunately, a convoy was on its way, guarded by an extraordinary number of battleships, aircraft carriers,

Above: the British crest

cruisers and destroyers. Many were lost en route but on 13 August 1942 *Port Chalmers*, *Melbourne Star* and *Rochester Castle* docked in Maltese waters. They were soon followed by the *Brisbane Star* and the tanker *Ohio*, which was carrying much-needed aviation fuel.

After their blockade of the islands was smashed, the Nazis intensified their concentration on North Africa, thereby reducing the pressure on Malta. In January 1943 the Allies took Tripoli and in May virtually all the soldiers in Germany's Afrika Korps – denied their means of escape across the Mediterranean by the tenacity of the Maltese – were taken prisoner.

Evidently impressed by their courage and valour, General Eisenhower sent the Maltese people the following supportive message: 'The epic of Malta is symbolic of the experience of the United Nations in this war; Malta has passed successively through the stages of woeful unpreparedness, tenacious endurance, intensive preparation and the initiation of a fierce offensive.' In May 1943, King George VI made a surprise visit to thank the islanders on behalf of Britain. Two months later the invasion of Sicily was launched from Malta. The surrender of the Italian fleet on 8 September signified the beginning of the end: Malta had survived its second great siege.

Mintoff's Socialist Alliances

After World War II the Maltese people faced a choice between independence, of which there was no shortage of advocates on the island, or union with the UK, with representation in the House of Commons. The islanders had the opportunity to decide for themselves in a referendum, but fewer than two-thirds of the population voted, and the British declared the result void. However, on 21 September 1964 Malta was granted independence within the Commonwealth, and on 13 December 1974, the island was declared a republic. The republican Dom Mintoff, who served as prime minister three times between 1971 and 1984, ruffled feathers on the island and internationally when he forged a series of alliances with socialist countries at a time when the Cold War was at its height. As a result, Mintoff's relationship with Whitehall was frequently fraught. The last British military base on the island closed in 1979.

Today, Malta is a Republic. The executive government is led by a prime

Above: an anti-aircraft gun in World War II
Right: Freedom Day. **Next Page:** Pretty Bay

minister while the legislative parliament is comprised of 65 members. The head of the republic is the president, whose role is largely ceremonial. Malta joined the Council of Europe in 1964. Under the ruling Labour Party its application to join the European Union in 1996 was frozen, but the Nationalists reinstated it in 1998 and, on 1 May 2004, the island joined the EU.

Growth of Tourism

In recent years tourism, for decades one of the island's biggest sources of income, has become a major industry. The five-star hotel sector – including conference and convention facilities – is booming, as is the development of leisure amenities and nightlife centres. Most of these are centred in Paceville and St George's Bay. Important tourist developments in progress include the Tigne and Manoel Island projects where apartment blocks surrounded by shopping complexes will stand alongside historic fortresses. Also under discussion are new yacht marinas in Gozo and St Paul's Bay. The renewal of the Valletta-Marsa Pinto Wharf area is partially completed with a terminal for cruise liner passengers currently in the pipeline.

A number of sophisticated technological industries reflect the high priority given to technology in the island's secondary and further education syllabuses, a policy augmented by specialised apprenticeship schemes and the university's excellent engineering faculty. In the 1990s, the Maltese government embarked on privatisation schemes intended to liberalise a number of sectors – banking, insurance, telecommunications, the port, the airport, popular state lotteries – that were previously state-run. Much legislation aligning Malta with EU standards has been introduced. Membership of the EU has ensured the islands are very much a part of Europe with their own members in the European Parliament in Brussels.

For all their sleepy image, Malta and Gozo are striding ahead confidently. Internet and mobile phone use are among the highest in Europe, a cable TV network transmits 60 international news, features and sports channels, and every year more satellite dishes appear on the skyline. A third casino, the Casino di Venezia, stands proudly on the Cottonera front, and all-night discos, salsa and tango bars are more popular than ever. Not that modern entertainment has supplanted the locals' traditional, Christian way of life: the village fiestas present the spirit of Malta as much as they ever did.

HISTORY HIGHLIGHTS

Pre-5 million BC Malta is part of land mass joining Europe to Africa.

5000 BC Neolithic Age; Red and Grey Skorba period; temple of Ta'Hagrat built.

4000–3000 BC The Copper Age; megalithic temples built at Ggantija, Tarxien, Hagar Qim and Mnajdra.

2500–900 BC The Bronze Age; Borg in-Nadur inhabited. The Hypogeum Burial Chamber excavated over a period of 500 years.

675–600 BC Phoenician colonisation.

480 BC Carthaginian domination.

264 BC First Punic War.

218 BC Malta incorporated into the Republic of Rome.

AD 60 St Paul, shipwrecked on Malta, converts Publius to Christianity.

330 Byzantine rule begins.

533 Belisarius, Justinian's general, establishes a port on Malta.

870 The Aghlabid Caliphs conquer the island. Their language forms the basis for the *il Malti* spoken today.

1091 Arabs routed by Christian forces of Sicilian-based Roger the Norman.

1266–83 Angevin dynasty rules.

1283–1530 The Spanish Aragonese dominate life on Malta.

1530 The Order of St John takes possession of the islands.

1561 The Inquisition is established.

1565 The Great Siege.

1566 Founding of Valletta.

1693 An earthquake destroys many historic buildings on the islands.

1798 Napoleon conquers Malta; the Order of St John leaves the island: the Inquisition is abolished.

1799 The Maltese rise against French domination. Britain offers the islands its protection.

1800 French force capitulates.

1802 Maltese Declaration of Rights asks that the islands come under the protection of the British Crown.

1814 Treaty of Paris; Malta becomes a British Crown Colony.

1914–18 World War I: A destination for wounded troops, Malta is known as the 'Nurse of the Mediterranean'.

1921 Granted self-government over domestic affairs, the first Maltese parliament is convened

1930 The Maltese constitution is suspended because of Church interference. It is restored two years later, but again suspended in 1933. Political unrest ensues.

1936 Constitution is amended: executive council members nominated.

1940 First Maltese civilian casualties of World War II – killed by air raids.

1942 Second Great Siege; George Cross awarded to the island for bravery.

1947 Self-government is restored.

1964 Malta becomes an independent state within British Commonwealth.

1972 An agreement is signed with Britain and NATO allowing the use of the islands as a military base.

1974 Malta becomes a republic, but remains within British Commonwealth.

1979 Last British forces leave.

1989 US President Bush and Soviet leader Gorbachev meet for the Malta Summit in Marsaxlokk to mark end of Cold War.

1992 Queen Elizabeth II visits the islands where she dedicates the World War II Siege Bell Memorial.

1996 Labour Party withdraws application to join European Union.

1998 Nationalists regain power, led by Dr Eddie Fenech Adami. They re-open application for EU membership.

2001 Pope John Paul II visits Malta to beatify Dun Gorg Preca, Adeodata Pisani and Nazju Falzon, who become the first Maltese to be beatified by the Roman Catholic Church.

2004 Malta becomes member of the EU on 1 May.

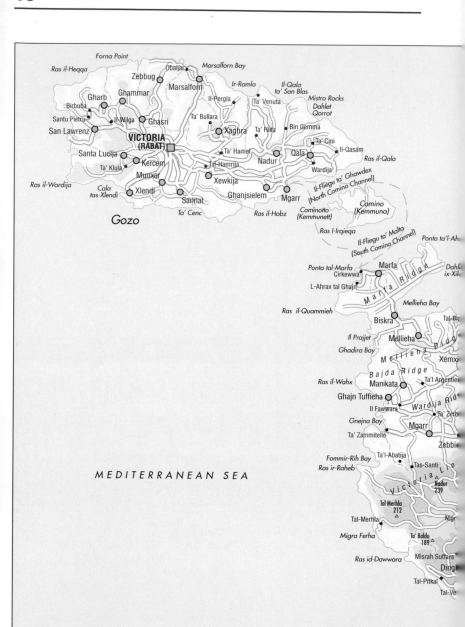

The Maltese Islands

3 km / 5 miles

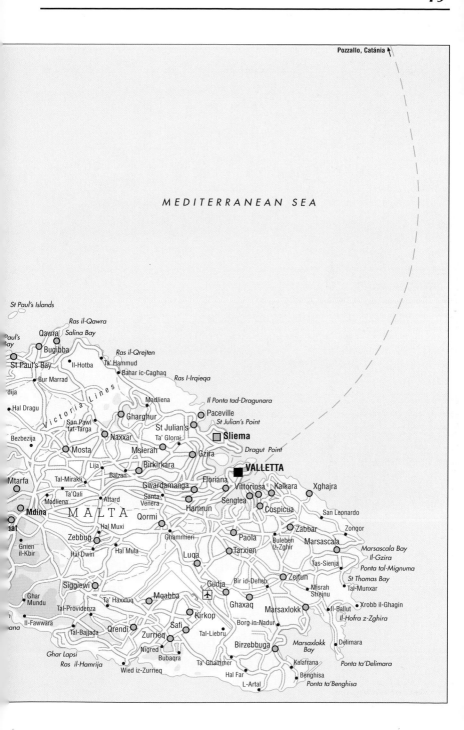

Pozzallo, Catánia

MEDITERRANEAN SEA

St Paul's Islands

Ras il-Qawra

Paul's
ay

Qawra / Salina Bay

Bugibba

St Paul's Bay

Il-Hotba

Ta' Hammud

Ras il-Qrejten

Bahar ic-Caghaq

Bur Marrad

Ras I-Irqieqa

dija

Hal Dragu

Madliena

Il Ponta tad-Dragunara

Victoria Lines

San Pawl
tat-Targa

Gharghur

Paceville

St Julian's Point

Bezbezija

Naxxar

St Julian's

Ta' Glorni

Sliema

Mosta

Msierah

Gzira

Dragut Point

Lija

Birkirkara

Mtarfa

Tal-Mirakli

Balzan

VALLETTA

Ta'Qali

Gwardamanga

Floriana

Vittoriosa

Kalkara

Xghajra

Madliena

Attard

Santa
Venera

Senglea

Mdina

M A L T A

Qormi

Hamrun

Cospicua

San Leonardo

Hal Muxi

Zabbar

Zongor

Zebbug

Ghammieri

Paola

Buleben
iz-Zghir

Marsascala

Gnien
il-Kbir

Hal Dwin

Hal Mula

Luqa

Tarxien

Marsascala Bay
Il-Gzira

Tas-Sienja

Ponta tal-Mignuma

Siggiewi

Gudja

Bir id-Deheb

Zejtun

St Thomas Bay

Ghar
Mundu

Ta' Haxxluq

Mqabba

Misrah
Strejnu

Tal-Munxar

Tal-Providenza

Ghaxaq

Marsaxlokk

Xrobb il-Ghagin

Il-Ballut

Il-Fawwara

Kirkop

Borg in-Nadur

Il-Hofra z-Zghira

ana

Tal-Bajjada

Qrendi

Safi

Tal-Liebru

Zurrieq

Migred

Birzebbuga

Marsaxlokk
Bay

Delimara

Ghar Lapsi

Ras il-Hamrija

Bubaqra

Ta' Ghammer

Kalafrana

Ponta ta'Delimara

Wied iz-Zurrieq

Hal Far

Benghisa

Ponta ta'Benghisa

L-Artal

Malta
Itineraries

1. THE KNIGHTS' CITY *(see map, p22)*

A day's exploration of the historic city of Valletta. Stroll down Republic Street then enjoy a light lunch at Caffè Cordina on Republic Square, or dine more elegantly at Ambrosia or Rubino (booking essential). Circumnavigate the city's bastions in the afternoon.

Get off the bus at the terminal between Triton Fountain and City Gate; or park the car in the large car park in Floriana, facing the Hotel Le Meridien Phoenicia. Or use the new (sign-posted) Park-and-Ride system, open in 2006. Each half of this itinerary takes about three hours.

Valletta is a living work of art despite the advent of ugly electrical wires and TV aerials. The houses and shop facades sport the ubiquitous enclosed wooden balconies that are so characteristic of the city. The balconies blend gracefully with the golden sandstone of the buildings.

Pausing outside the **City Gate**, you will notice the former moat below. Dug by Turkish slaves, and measuring 17 metres (55ft) deep by 9 metres (29ft) wide, the moat extends for 875 metres (2,840ft) between the two harbours. Once a protective barrier, it's now a car park. Of greater benefit to pedestrians is **Republic Street**. Bisecting the city, it runs approximately 2km (1 mile) to Fort St Elmo and is off-limits to motorists, but be wary of traffic zooming across the road from the side streets. If you need a **tourist office** there is one just to the right of the arcade's entrance. The ruins in the large square are those of the Royal Opera House, which was bombed in 1942.

At South Street, a left turn brings you to St Andrew's Scottish Church, then the **National Museum of Fine Arts** (open daily 9am–5pm), between Old Mint and Vassalli streets. This excellent museum features a magnificent collection of paintings of Malta throughout the last 500 years. Back on Republic Street, **St Barbara's**, designed by Giuseppe Bonnici, is the parish church serving the foreign community, with masses in English, Spanish, French and German. Originally the church of the Langue of Provence, this bright and intimate church is oval in shape with a domed ceiling. On the other side of the street, the pale green interior of **St Francis's church** provides a soothing contrast.

Prehistoric Temples

A little way further down on the left, the **Auberge of Provence** houses the **Museum of Archaeology** (open daily 9am–5pm), whose exhibits include models of the prehistoric temples of Ggantija, Mnajdra, Hagar Qim and Tarxien. Among the archaeological finds displayed here are the original of the Fertility Goddess found in Tarxien. Some say that the museum's

Left: the Grand Harbour
Right: knights played a key role in Maltese history

finest feature is the building itself – it is the only one of the Knights' original auberges (taverns) that is open to the public. Begun in 1571, it was designed by the renowned Valletta architect, Gerolamo Cassar.

On leaving the museum, walk along Melita Street to Zachary, then turn left to take in the magnificence of **St John's Co-Cathedral**. The facade is plain, the buttressing hidden behind it. A bronze bust of Christ by Alessandro Algardi is in the pediment, and above it is a Maltese Cross, the symbol of the Order of St John. The cathedral, designed by Cassar, was consecrated on 20 February 1578: until 1798 it was the order's conventual church. Pope Pius VII gave it the title co-cathedral in 1816 to resolve the rivalry between Mdina and Valletta which dated back to the Knights' arrival in 1530.

It is difficult to imagine a more startling contrast than that between the church's exterior and its interior. Whereas the outside is austere, the inside is artfully and richly decorated. Rectangular in shape, the church features a barrelled interior with chapels on either side of the central chamber. The buttressing which Cassar hid with his exterior walls separates the main body of the church from the side altars. The interior is best seen when empty, when the full sweep of some 400 floor sepulchre slabs can be appreciated.

Tombs of the Grand Masters

The bronze lecterns, dated 1557, came from the Knights' chapter church in Vittoriosa. The high altar, finished in 1686, is of lapis lazuli and in its centre is a bronze bas relief of the *Last Supper*. Giuseppe Mazzuoli created the large marble group, the *Baptism of Christ*, at the end of the chancel. Seven of the eight original members of the order have their own chapel dedicated to the patron saint of their Langue and containing the tombs of the grand masters. The missing member is England; as a result of Henry VIII's fight with Rome the English Knights were withdrawn from the order.

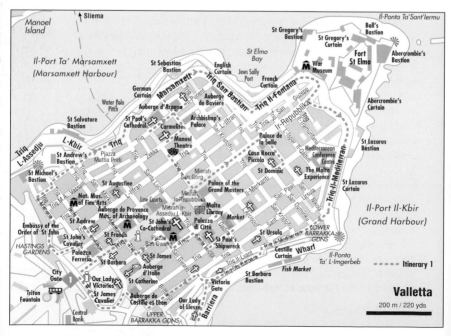

The cathedral ceiling was bare until Mattia Preti was commissioned in 1661 to decorate it. The greatest treasure in the oratory leading to the **Cathedral Museum** (entrance through the third arch on the right) is a painting by Caravaggio, *The Beheading of St John the Baptist*. The museum houses a fine collection of Flemish tapestries, silver objects and sacred vestments.

On leaving St John's, turn left on **Merchants' Street**, and browse through the goods in the market; take a right at St Lucia, then a left on St Paul's Street to reach **St Paul's Shipwreck Church**. The **Covered Market** in the next block is set in a graceful Victorian structure that was renovated in the late 1980s. Walk through the market and across the street you will see the rear of the Palace of the Grand Masters. Pass through the arcade to your left: Republic Square is at the end on the left.

The large building at the back is the **Biblioteca**, the national library, designed by the Sicilian architect Stefano Ittar in 1786. A statue of Queen Victoria stands in front of it, surrounded by the tables of three outdoor cafés. The most famous of these, the **Caffè Cordina**, was established in 1837. Check out **Great Siege Square** a block back up Republic Street towards the city gate. The large monument here is dedicated to the defenders of Malta who died during the Great Siege.

Commendations from George VI and Roosevelt

In Palace Square, the 45-minute Great Siege of Malta attraction uses state-of-the-art technology and is well worth a visit. The exterior of the **Palace of the Grand Masters** in **Palace Square** is covered with plaques commemorating historical events, including the citation King George VI wrote when he awarded the island the George Cross in 1942, and a letter from the American President Franklin Roosevelt commending the islanders for their valour. The grand masters used the palace as their headquarters until they left the island in 1798. During the British colonial period it was the governor's headquarters. Since 1974 it has served as the office of the president.

Signs outside the palace point towards the entrance on the right, but ignore them, and walk through the **Prince of Wales entrance** to enter **Neptune's Court**, with

Above: St John's Co-Cathedral
Right: Neptune in the court named after him

malta itineraries

its subtropical plants. **Prince Alfred's Court**, named in honour of a visit by Queen Victoria's second son in 1858, is through an archway to the right. The clock dates from 1745; the hours are struck by figures representing Moorish slaves.

To reach the public entrance to the **State Apartments** (open daily 10am–5pm) visitors must use an entrance at the rear, in Merchants Street. Unfortunately, visitors are not allowed to climb the massive stone steps the Knights once used but, once on the first floor, you can see them through the glass doors to the left. The Knights used the **Tapestry Room** (first left) as their council chamber, and this is where the Maltese parliament – meeting between 1921 and 1976 – established the republican government. The tapestries in the first chamber to the left were given to the order by Grand Master Perellos in the 18th century. The friezes above the tapestries depict the Knights' galleys in battle against the Turks.

Great Siege Frescoes

The **Throne Room**, the Knights' Hall of St Michael and St George, contains the Great Siege frescoes, although you would need a pair of binoculars to study them properly. Painted between 1576 and 1581, they portray the battles from the Turks' arrival at Marsaxlokk Bay until their eventual withdrawal. The small balcony on the wall opposite the throne was made from the stern

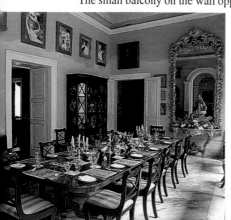

of the *Grand Carrick of Rhodes*, Grand Master Adam's flagship. The **Armoury** is on the ground floor at the rear, near the Neptune courtyard. It contains one of the finest collections of weaponry in Europe, including a gold Damascene suit of armour fashioned for Grand Master Aloph de Wignacourt.

Further down Old Theatre Street is **Manoel Theatre**. Financed by Grand Master Manoel de Vilhena 'for the honest

Above: Palace of the Knights
Left: Casa Rocca Piccola

recreation of the people', it opened in 1732. Beautifully restored in 1969, it is believed to be the second oldest theatre in use in Europe. Plays are staged in English and Maltese; tours are offered during the week, tickets from the box office. Back on Republic Street, **Casa Rocca Piccola** at No 74 is the only historical home of a Maltese noble family open to the public (tours last about 30 minutes). The house was originally owned by the Langue of Italy, and was built soon after the Knights moved their headquarters to Valletta. It was restored by the present marquis and has some of the oldest examples of Maltese furniture. In the library is a set of 17th-century canvases said to have adorned Grand Master Lascari's barge. In the Blue Sitting Room you can see surgical instruments used in the Knights' Hospital.

The Last Supper

Situated between St Dominic and St Nicholas streets, the late 16th-century **Palace de la Salle** has a beautiful balcony, and was the home of Grand Master Ramon Perellos. Turn right on St Nicholas and again at Merchants' Street to reach **St Dominic's Church**. During Easter week, this is one of the places where the Last Supper is re-created. The morning walk ends here. For lunch, try Caffè Cordina on Republic Square or, if you have booked, head for Ambrosia or Rubino then on to the bastions that form the focus of the afternoon itinerary.

Standing once more inside the City Gate, take a left on Ordinance Street, then another to get on to the bastions and Pope Pius V Street. A short walk to the left takes you to the top of the City Gate. To your left is **Hastings Gardens**, built on St John's Bastion and named after a former governor of the island. The gardens, which continue until St Michael's Bastion, offer wonderful views over Marsamxett Harbour, Manoel Island and Tigne Point. The same views are available a little lower down, from **St Andrew's Bastion**. The balconies on St Andrew's Street are some of the city's finest.

The Sliema ferry leaves from the foot of St Mark's Street. If you are waiting for a ferry you can enjoy a drink with locals at the **Cockney Bar**. Look out for the water-polo pitch in the sea.

St Paul's Anglican Cathedral has a tall steeple – the dome resembling St Paul's Cathedral in London is that of the nearby Carmelite Church. Take the steps beside it to explore both. St Paul's serves Malta's Anglican community; the interior is highlighted with the banner and crest of Queen Adelaide, the widow of King William IV and benefactor of the church. Built from local limestone, the interior matches the exterior in simplicity. The memorial on **Piazza Indipendenza** commemorates the citizens of Valletta killed in the 1799 rebellion against the French. The **Auberge d'Aragon**, one of the eight buildings designed by Gerolamo Cassar for the Langues of the Knights, is now

Right: the dome of the Carmelite Church looks like that of St Paul's in London

part of the Ministry for Economic Services. Nearby, on West Street, is the elegant facade of the **Our Lady of Pilar Church** (1670).

The **Carmelite Church** is one block up, its entrance on Old Mint Street. It replaced the church built in 1573 by Cassar, which was reduced to rubble during World War II. Returning to Piazza Indipendenza, the steps by the red postbox take you back to the road. Continuing to the right, you will find yourself on top of the **German Curtain**. When the road makes a sharp right you will reach **St Sebastian's Bastion** and the **Gun Post Snack Bar.** The latter is a particularly good place for views of Marsamxett Harbour.

The **Bavarian Auberge**, built in 1695, is between West and St Charles streets, directly above the Jews' Sally Port, which is located in the middle of the **English Curtain**; the **French Curtain** follows, and at the end the **War Museum** is tucked into a corner of **Fort St Elmo**. The museum's prize exhibit is the George Cross. The rest of its exhibits, including numerous photographs illustrating the destruction of the Three Cities (Senglea, Cospicua and Vittoriosa) and Valletta, chronicle the island's role in World War II.

The World's Longest Hospital Ward

Crossing the end of **Republic Street**, the **Mediterranean Conference Centre** sits just around the curve of Spur Street. Originally called the Sacra Infermeria (Holy Infirmary) of the Order of the Knights of St John of Jerusalem, its construction began in 1574, and continued over the next century until it eventually reached 153 metres (502ft) in length. It became the world's longest hospital ward, described as 'the grandest interior in the world'.

Nursing care here was the most advanced in Europe: at a time when a stint in hospital could mean death from infection, the Knights' hospital pioneered hygienic procedures. The School of Anatomy and Surgery, established in 1676 by Grand Master Cottoner, was the precursor of Malta's Medical School. During World War II parts of the building were destroyed and it was not until 1978 that it was returned to its former glory. Indeed, it won an award for restoration work. Today it is used as a convention centre, and can accommodate up to 1,400 delegates. Nearby there are hourly performances (11am–4pm) of the **Malta Experience**, a 40-minute multimedia show featuring commentary in five languages.

The Greek-looking temple dominating the nearby skyline is a World War II memorial, dedicated by Elizabeth II in 1992, 50 years after the island was awarded the George Cross. Up the hill the **Lower Barrakka Gardens** perch on **St Christopher's Bastion**. The small temple is a memorial to Sir Alexander Ball, a hero of the British blockade against Napoleon. The Three Cities are across the Grand Harbour and below to the right is the old **fish market**, which dates from 1643, when it was used to quarantine passengers.

Above: Lower Barrakka Gardens. **Above Right:** St Barbara's Bastion
Right: the Auberge de Castille and Lyons, now the prime minister's Office

You are about to arrive at one of the most beautiful, but unheralded, streets in Valletta. **St Barbara's Bastion** is not signposted, but at the end of St Lucy Curtain, a little street leads off to the left. A sign indicates a dead end, but if you walk down this street you will come across a series of classic Maltese homes, all neatly painted. One of these, the **Conservatorio Vincenzo Bugeja**, has elaborate balconies. At night, there is a wonderful view from here of the illuminated bastion of Fort St Angelo and the yacht marina.

Operation Husky

A sharp turn left at the end of the street leads downhill through Victoria Gate. The tunnel built into the bastion at the bottom of the hill is named after Grand Master Lascaris, as are the **Lascaris War Rooms**. Their entrance is next to the tourist office just inside the city. Here one can see where Operation Husky, the invasion of Sicily in July 1943, was planned.

Retrace your steps up **Liesse Hill**. Inside Victoria Gate climb the steps to the **Upper Barrakka Gardens**, which have a great view over the Grand Harbour. You will notice *Merhba* (welcome) spelt out in shrubs. Leaving the garden, you will see the **Auberge de Castille and Lyons**, now the prime minister's Office, and one of the most graceful buildings of the Maltese baroque period. A monument to the socialist Manuel Dimech graces the centre of Castille Place. The **Our Lady of Victories** in Valletta church next to the statue was the first building erected by the Knights to thank God for deliverance from the Turks. From Castille Place, **St James's Bastion** leads past the Central Bank of Malta to the **St James Cavalier** arts and exhibitions centre. Just ahead is City Gate, where the walk around the walls ends.

malta itineraries

2. RABAT, MDINA AND AN AFTERNOON CRUISE *(see map below)*

A leisurely stroll through the bustling streets of Mdina's suburb of Rabat, then through the heart of Malta's medieval 'Silent City'. Choose from three lunch options then cruise around Valletta's Grand Harbour.

Taken together, these morning walks can be done in half a day. Take a bus to Rabat or drive to Mdina's main gate; go early to get a parking space.

As a prelude to an exploration of Mdina, 'the Silent City', this itinerary goes first to its suburb of **Rabat**. The first port of call is the **Domus Romana**, (open 9am–4.30pm) situated at the end of Museum Road beyond **Howard Gardens**. This is the most important of the area's Roman remains. Formerly the villa of a wealthy citizen, its foundations were discovered in 1881. The villa has been recently restored with great style.

Parish Square hosts a small market every morning, with a far bigger one taking its place on Sunday. Flower-sellers jostle with vegetable stall-holders and some produce is still sold direct from horse-drawn carts. **St Paul's Church**, founded in 1575, and rebuilt by Lorenzo Gafa following the earthquake of 1693, stands on Parish Square. The church's main altar was designed by Mattia Preti; the painting above it of St Paul's shipwreck is by Stefano Erardi. The entrance to the **Grotto** is to the right of the main chapter door. According to legend, St Paul lived here during the three months he was on Malta. The walls of the cave are said to possess mystical healing powers.

Signposts point the way towards Rabat's three **catacombs** – **St Cataldus**, **St Paul's** and **St Agatha's**. They are typical of early, underground Christian tombs which were also used as places of worship. St Agatha's is a fairly long walk from Parish Square, but it is worth making the effort because these are the most interesting and beautiful of Rabat's catacombs. Be warned that the tun-

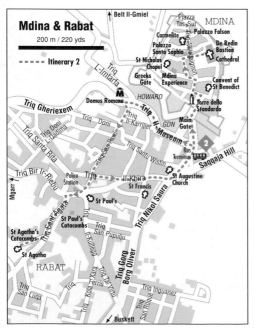

nels are very dark – it's a good idea to bring a torch. The frescoes in the grotto chapel detail the life of St Agatha, who fled her native Sicily rather than marry the pagan Quintanus, who was the Roman governor of Catania. She returned to Catalina where she suffered a martyr's fate as one of the victims of the emperor Decius's persecution.

The First Hospital

Retrace your steps to Parish Square, and take the pedestrian walk though the churchyard. Note a memorial marker attesting to Paul's admiration of the Maltese people, which is printed in eight languages. Turn right on Main Street and follow it to **Nikol Saura**

Road where **St Augustine's** church is just around the corner. Built in 1571 by Cassar, this building has a beautiful facade and a gilded barrel-vaulted interior. A block to the right is the first hospital to be built on the island, **Santo Spirito**, which was constructed in the mid-14th century and which continued to serve members of the public until 1968.

Mdina, whose city gate is but a short walk to the left, is known as Malta's 'Silent City'. Situated about 11km (7 miles) inland to the west of Valletta, it is one of the best-preserved medieval cities in the world. As you approach the city gate, you will doubt-less see lines of *karozzini*, Maltese carriages, for hire. They are an enjoyable form of trans-port by which to see Mdina, but not if you want to explore the city in your own time. Agree on the ride's price and duration before you set off.

malta itineraries

Bronze Age Villages

The distinctive silhouette of Mdina looms over the landscape from every part of the island. Situated at 154 metres (500ft) above sea level, it is Malta's high-est, most defensible point and was therefore the logical location for an early settlement. There were Bronze Age villages here, and during the Roman era, Mdina and Rabat, at that time one city, was the island's capital. The Aghlabid Arabs built the defensive ditch that bisects the city in the late 9th century, and it was they who named the fortified part *il-Medina* (The Fortified). The Normans, who retained Mdina as their capital, strengthened the fortifications and built magnificent churches and palaces.

The arrival of the Knights in 1530 transformed the status of Mdina. The Knights, whose power base was the small town of Birgu (today's Vittoriosa), assumed positions of leadership. With the building of Valletta, Mdina became known as *Citta Vecchia* (Old City). During the era of British sovereignty Mdina was no longer a centre of power, but it remained the home of Malta's noble families. Today it is a fine example of a walled medieval city. The houses have been maintained by their owners, the churches by the faithful, and Mdina remains a place of serene repose – hence its nickname, the Silent City.

The torches placed beside the doors of numer-ous houses are replicas of medieval street lights. Mdina is famed for its elaborate door-knockers and the grillework that covers the windows of many a smart residence.

A short road over a defensive moat (now filled with volleyball and tennis courts) leads through the **Main**

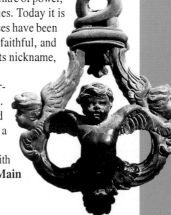

Above: time to talk in Rabat
Right: attractive twist on a Mdina door-knocker

Gate into **St Publius Square**, named in honour of Malta's first Christian, who also became one of its patron saints (St Paul and St Agatha are the others). Inside, **Torre dello Standardo** sits on the left; at one time fires were lit on the roof of the tower to warn the population when an enemy was approaching. To the right of it, the **Mdina Dungeons**, located in the Corte Capitanale, satisfy lovers of all things gory with graphic exhibits of torture and persecution.

Of a more peaceful disposition, the **Museum of Natural History** (next right; open daily 9am–5pm) is housed in the Palazzo Vilhena, an enchanting old building with a delightful courtyard. The original building on this site, destroyed by an earthquake in 1693, was the seat of the Università, Malta's original governing body.

Villegaignon Street, named after the French knight who defended Mdina from the Turks in 1551, starts to the left and ends at Bastion Square. On the right corner is the chapel dedicated to St Agatha, built in 1417 and renovated by Lorenzo Gafa in 1694. Opposite is the Casa Inguanez, home of Malta's oldest family. If you want to take advantage of the **Mdina Experience**, a wonderful combination of slides and commentary tracing Mdina's history, take **Mesquita Street** to the square.

Resistance HQ

Two buildings on **St Paul's Square** beside the cathedral stand out: the Victorian Gothic **Casa Gourgin** and, opposite it, the **Banca Giuratale** (now the Magistrates' House), built by Vilhena for the Università. During the revolt against the French in 1798, the Banca became the legislative headquarters of the resistance leaders. But it is the **Cathedral of St Paul** upon which all eyes come to rest. Its site is historic: the home of St Publius is reputed to have stood here, and before Roger I, the Norman Count of Sicily, constructed a church here at the beginning of the 12th century, several others had stood in the same place. Roger's church was destroyed by the 1693 earthquake, which left only the apse standing. When construction of the present church was started in 1697, the apse was incorporated into the structure.

Built in the shape of a Latin cross, the cathedral interior is sumptuous. The memorial tablets in the nave resemble those in St John's in Valletta: both demonstrate a combination of the macabre and the angelic. Vincenzo and Antonio Manno

Above: Mdina's Main Gate
Right: the Museum of Natural History

created the frescoes on the ceiling; commissioned in 1794, they detail scenes from the life of St Paul. In the north transept, look out for Mattia Preti's painting of St Paul saving the Maltese people from Saracen invaders in 1422.

According to local legend, the cathedral's silver processional cross accompanied Godfrey de Bouillon when he entered Jerusalem at the culmination of the First Crusade. In the shrine to the left of the main altar is an icon of the Madonna, reputedly painted by St Luke, but which is more likely to be Byzantine. The **Cathedral Museum** (open daily 9am–5pm), on the right side of Archbishop's Square, opposite the cathedral's entrance, features a number of items rescued from the 1693 earthquake, 15th-century Sicilian panels that decorated the cathedral's choir, and some superb Dürer woodcuts.

Mdina's Oldest House

The **Carmelite Church**, sitting at the corner of St Peter Street, is a baroque jewel with an exquisitely painted oval dome. The **Palazzo Santa Sophia**, which straddles St Sophia Street, is reputedly the oldest house in Mdina, with a cornerstone dating it back to 1388. The view from the expansive, open **Bastion Square** that looms ahead is terrific. When there are no clouds or mist, Mount Etna on Sicily is clearly visible. The dome straight ahead belongs to **Mosta's Church of the Assumption** *(see Itinerary 3, page 34)*. At night, a fairy-tale picture of urban lights matches the sky in brilliance.

For lunch there are several good options. You might want to enjoy a picnic on the bastion, or you could stroll down Bastion Street to the **Fontenella Tea Garden** for a snack. Alternatively, if you are really hungry, retrace your steps to Holy Cross Street for something grander at the **Medina Restaurant**. After lunch, drive or take a taxi back across the island to the Strand in **Sliema** (opposite Valletta) where boats leave between 10am and 4pm for a cruise through Marsamxett and Grand harbours. Each cruise takes about 75 minutes with commentary in English, French and German.

Above: Mdina is one of the world's best examples of a walled, medieval city

The large yacht repair yard on the other side of Sliema Creek is situated on **Manoel Island**, currently being developed with high-rise apartments and shopping precincts. Previously known as Bishop Island, this small piece of land once served as a quarantine centre. The graceful, arched **Lazaretto of San Rocco**, built around 1640 and renovated in the following century, is one of the hospitals where incoming passengers were detained if suspected of carrying bubonic plague. The ruins of **Fort Manoel** crown the slight hill.

The boat makes a slight dip into **Lazaretto Creek** to see the yacht basin before swinging around the peninsula of Ta'Xbiex and heading into **Marsamxett Harbour**; notice the little 'thumb' of water, called Pieta Creek. There's a Gozo cargo ferry here which departs from the Sa Maison Bastion.

As the boat cruises through Marsamxett Harbour, other Valletta bastions rise from the water to your right. As the ship rounds the corner heading toward Fort St Elmo, the English Curtain is visible. On the promontory opposite is **Tigne Point** and **Fort Tigne**, the latter built in 1761 to serve, along with Fort St Elmo, as guardian of Marsamxett Harbour (Tigne Point, like Manoel Island, is being turned into a residential estate).The massive bulk of **Fort St Elmo** hovers above; it's now the Malta Police Academy and home to the National War Museum. In 1565 it was the Knights' first line of defence against the Ottomans in the Great Siege.

Three Peninsulas

The headland on the left as you enter the **Grand Harbour** is topped by **Ricasoli Fort**. **Bighi** occupies the tip of the second peninsula and **Fort St Angelo** is at the head of the third, on a site that has been continuously occupied since Phoenician times. After Fort St Elmo fell in the Great Siege, Fort St Angelo bore the full brunt of the Ottoman attack, but the walls stood firm. Today, the fort is being restored by the Knights of St John.

Tug boats are berthed at the head of the creek, next to the South Gate Dry Docks. The district of **Senglea** fills the last 'finger'. **St Michael's Fort**, also an important cornerstone in the Knights' defences against the Turks, stood here, but much of it, along with Senglea itself, was destroyed in the

course of Axis bombings in World War II. From St Michael's Fort there are fantastic views of Valletta.

The final sight on this side of the Grand Harbour is of the **Malta Dry Docks**, which are easily recognised by the enormous cranes that rise into the sky like an enormous piece of modern installation art. During World War II the docks were subjected to the most intense bombardment in world history, which went on for a terrifying 69 consecutive days.

The boat turns round here – Valletta is now on your left – and makes its way back to base at Sliema.

Left: cruising around the harbours

3. A CENTRAL CIRCLE *(see map, p34)*

Explore the gardens of San Anton Palace; shop for souvenirs and gifts at the Ta'Qali Crafts Village; see Mosta's church dome; and conclude the itinerary at St Helen's Church in the historic parish of Birkirkara.

This itinerary requires a car because no direct bus service links the towns.

From Valletta, take the road to Rabat. About 1.5km (1 mile) beyond Farson's Brewery, a small signpost points right towards **San Anton Gardens**. If you miss it, take the next right (almost immediately) and double back. San Anton Palace and gardens are a block off the main road.

San Anton Palace served as the country residence of the grand masters from the early 17th century. In the British colonial era it was used as the governor's residence. Since 1974 it has been the official home of the republic's president and so not open to visitors. The gardens display an astonishing assortment of subtropical trees. Walking in an anti-clockwise direction, the first feature you are bound to notice is the Eagle Fountain, which is adorned with cherubs.

Miniature Pagoda

Looking straight ahead you'll see the main central pond and the palace entrance. The nearest arch leads to an aviary, behind which is a miniature five-storey pagoda, presented by the Japan Cherry Blossom Foundation. The inviting terrace in front of the palace is backed by an ivy-covered wall. Two stone chairs flank the entrance. In the courtyard ahead the green doors on the right lead to the president's office.

Leaving San Anton Gardens, return to the main road and take a right towards Rabat. Be prepared for the right turn to **Ta'Qali** as soon as the National Stadium's floodlights come into view on the right. A **Crafts Village** is located on the World War II airfield. Pottery, lace-making, weaving, silverwork and glass-blowing are a few of the traditional Maltese crafts

Top: St Mary's Church, featuring the fourth largest unsupported dome in Europe
Right: the gardens of San Anton Palace, official home of the republic's president

demonstrated here. Mdina Glass is the best-known and largest business of its kind and it is fascinating to watch the craftsmen at work.

Exit the way you entered, but follow the signs to **Mosta**. When you arrive at the T-junction, turn left towards Rabat. At the next T, which joins the main road, take a right turn, and the dome of Mosta will be just ahead. This less travelled road brings you into Mosta by a more picturesque route. Follow the street into the centre of town. At the church square take a left and then a right to the church car park.

A Landmark Dome

Mosta's dome is a landmark throughout the island. Measuring 37 metres (122ft) in diameter, it is reputed to be the fourth largest unsupported dome in Europe, smaller only than the Pantheon, St Peter's in Rome and the Basilica at Xewkija in Gozo. Look up at the ceiling, which is decorated with a geometric diamond pattern. Some visitors are so taken by the dome that they neglect the rest of the church of **St Mary's**, which is a shame. This neoclassical building replaced one originally designed in 1614 by local architect Tomasso Dingli. In happy contrast to the rebuilding necessitated by wars and earthquakes, the church had to be redeveloped to accommodate the growth of the village. Designed by another local architect, Giorgio Grognet de Vasse, the construction of St Mary's was completed in 1860. In a **small museum** (open daily 9am–5pm) to the left of the right-hand altar there's a bomb that fell through the dome in 1942 without exploding or injuring anyone.

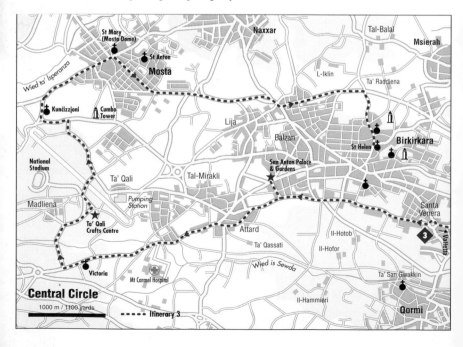

Central Circle

1000 m / 1100 yards

----- Itinerary 3

To reach the historic parish of **Birkirkara** (B'Kara on signs), take the road to Valletta. Ignore the 'B'Kara Centre' sign and go left on the bypass road (signposted St Julian's). At the second roundabout, take the third exit, fom which the dome and belfries of **St Helen's** are clearly visible, and park here. In 1436, Malta was deemed too large for two parishes (Mdina and Birgu), so 10 more, including Birkirkara, were established. In 1630, Pope Urban VIII issued a bull declaring Birkirkara the first collegiate parish on Malta. A more singular papal honour bestowed by Pius X in 1912 is seen during the parade to mark the Feast Day of St Helen (the Sunday following 18 August) when a liveried character carrying a silver mace precedes the cannons.

The present church stands on the site of an earlier one which was destroyed in the 1693 earthquake. The architect of St Helen's was Domenico Cachia, a local man. Completed in 1745, it is considered one of the finest examples of Maltese ecclesiastical architecture. Designed in a classic baroque Latin cross, the interior is 55 metres (180ft) long and 36 metres (117ft) wide, with a large dome over the main altar. The frescoes, completed between 1906 and 1910, depict scenes in the life of St Helen.

Head home the way you came to avoid Birkirkara's one-way streets.

4. THE THREE CITIES *(see map, p36)*

Travelling by bus or car, this itinerary comprises a four- to five-hour exploration of the small cities of Senglea, Cospicua and Vittoriosa.

Start near Senglea and finish at Bighi.

The Three Cities were originally called il-Birgu, l-Isla and Bormla. They were renamed Vittoriosa, Senglea and Cospicua respectively after the Great Siege. The fortifications that surround Cospicua are the result of several centuries of building in the wake of the siege. The Margherita Lines which ran from French Creek to Kalkara Creek were designed by Marculano da Firenzuloa in 1638; the Cottonera Lines outside them, which form a semi-circle with a circumference of 5km (3 miles) were built between 1670 and 1680. The two rings formed a secure line of defence in which over 40,000 people could be housed in times of war. Today most of the bastions are surrounded by apartment buildings and have had tunnels dug through them for traffic access.

From Sliema and Valletta drivers should follow signs to the airport and at the roundabout take the **Paola** exit (the first left). Stay on this road until the second roundabout, then take the **Cospicua** exit, drive through St Helen's Gate in the Margherita Bastions, and park on St Paul Square. To get into **Senglea**, walk along Triq Il-Mons. If travelling by bus to Senglea, ask the driver to let you off before **St Michael's Gate**.

Above Left: carrying the mace on the annual Feast Day of St Helen
Right: wrought-iron balconies look out over the small city of Senglea

Claude de la Sengle, after whom the city is named, fortified the walls in 1554 and built Fort St Michael. After Fort St Elmo fell during the Great Siege, Fort St Michael (dismantled in 1922), and Fort St Angelo became the primary targets of the Ottoman guns, and a great chain was stretched across the points of the 'fingers' with a bridge of boats that allowed the defenders to move men easily between the two. The peninsula was bombarded again during World War II when the nearby dry docks were a target.

Inside the gates, on the left, is **Our Lady of Victory Church**. The modern monument is dedicated to the Three Cities residents killed in 1940–43. Just beyond it, go left up the steps of **Triq San Pietru u San Pawl** and peer over the wall at the end for a direct look into the heart of the docks.

The Miracle Madonna

Return to the main street; on **Pjazza L-Erbgha Ta'Settembru** is a copy of the Madonna and Child statue which used to stand in front of Our Lady of Victory Church. This is often called the 'Miracle Madonna' because it remained unscathed by bombs. Stop for a moment and look at the pleasing pattern the balconies make as they lead the eye up Triq il-Vittorja towards the baroque **St Philip's Church** on Pjazza Francesco Zahra Pittur.

Turn right at the church then left on Triq Iz-Zewg Mini and you will soon arrive at the **Safe Haven Garden**, which has wonderful views over the harbour to Valletta. Here stands the **Vedette**, an old lookout point famous for its sculpted eyes and ears. (The pelican is a symbol of Christian love.) At the park entrance, descend the steps to the left for a walk round the point.

Throughout this walk, you are bound to see boat clubs where members work on their *dghajsas* – the distinctive boats reminiscent of Venetian gondolas and decorated in bright colours. Today they feature in annual boat races but there was a time when they worked as ferries, transporting people between the towns that surround the Grand Harbour.

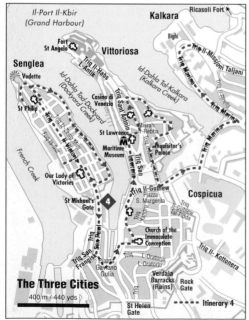

The Three Cities

Retrace your steps around the tip. Towards the head of the bay, stepped streets lead steeply upwards; both the **Alice Springs** and **Prince Charles** kiosks are good for a snack or a cold drink. The archway ahead signals the end of Senglea. The old dry docks don't let you walk by the water's edge yet, so you will need to go back to San Pawl Square and continue downhill to Gavino Gulia Square and the bus terminal (if you're ready to call it a day). The dry docks are to be developed as a tourist destination.

Cospicua was Malta's worst casualty in World War II: over 90 percent of the town was flattened. Unfortunately, rebuilding has not

been undertaken with much care. Around the curve of the bay, several flights of steps lead to the **Church of the Immaculate Conception**. Nearby is **Maxim's**, where you can get virtually any variety of the local speciality: cheesecake. Down the hill and back on the main road, cross to the left (water) side and follow the walls. Here the Bormla Boat and Regatta Club welcomes visitors.

The Last British Base

At the crest of the hill is **Vittoriosa**, the first Sicilian-Norman capital, known in medieval times as Birgu. When the Knights arrived in 1530, they made Birgu their base. After the Great Siege, the city was renamed Vittoriosa, but when the Knights moved to their new capital, Valletta, the power structure went with them. At the end of the street into Vittoriosa, palm trees surround the four statues of the monument which commemorates the closing of the last British base in 1979. Before exploring the church of St Lawrence behind it, visit the **Maritime Museum** (Open daily 9am–5pm), in a former Royal Navy bakery. Further along the waterfront with its yacht marina capable of

birthing the world's largest private yachts as well as small craft, the architectural gem known as Scamp's Palace has been converted into the Casino di Venezia.

Leaving the Maritime Museum, walk towards **Fort St Angelo** which, after a period of disintegration, is being restored to its past glory – and for possible future use as a museum. From here there are wonderful views over the Grand Harbour.

Go back to the square fronting the church of **St Lawrence**, the first conventual church of the order, which contains many relics of the Knights. Built in 1691, the church shares with the **Oratorio of St Joseph**

Above: the Three Cities' 'fingers'
Right: the Vedette lookout point

(located at the rear) the site of Santo Maria Damascene where the Knights used to worship. The steps to the left lead to St Joseph and then into **Victory Square**. The Knights' Auberge d'Allemagne is situated on the corner of the square at Triq Hilda Tabone (also called Britannic); next to it is the Auberge d'Angleterre; the Auberge d'Auvergne et de Provence is opposite. Several buildings up is the Auberge de France, with a portal by Bartolomeo Genga.

Return to Victory Square and, if you want to go directly to the Inquisitor's Palace, leave the square via Triq Il-Mina L-Kbira (Main Gate). To explore

more of Vittoriosa before seeing the palace, take Triq San Filippu at the northwest corner of the square, then at the end of it go down the steps by the red postbox. At the bottom is a field where *bocci* is played. *Bocci* is a Maltese form of boule (which is popular throughout the Mediterranean) that features solid cylindrical pieces of wood rather than wooden or metal balls. The bar beneath the *bocci* field serves cold drinks.

Follow the wall up the hill until you arrive at **Triq il-Manolragg**, which marks the end of a series of good views. At the square, take the road going right and follow it to Triq Il-Kwartier, which leads into Triq Pacifiku Scicluna; at the end, go left on to Triq Papa Alessandru. Where this ends, turn right on to Triq Il-Palazz Ta'L-Isqof, the entrance to the **Inquisitor's Palace** is on the right.

The Inquisition, or Holy Office, was established in Malta in 1562, with the role of protecting the Catholic faith by any means. Of the island's 62 inquisitors, two became popes, and 22 attained the cardinal's red hat. The inquisitors beat a hasty retreat when the French conquered the island in 1798. In the 19th century the palace was used as officers' quarters. The present building was constructed in the 1530s and, although the interior has not been properly furnished, the timbered ceilings are among the best on the island. The dungeons are situated beneath the public rooms.

Leave Vittoriosa via the **Gate of Provence**, and return to your car (or wait for a bus at the nearby stop), or turn left and continue down the hill. The latter means leaving the Three Cities, but tiny **Kalkara** is definitely worth seeing. The large church which sits at the head of Kalkara Creek is the beautifully austere **St Joseph**. The main sanctuary is made of local sandstone. The altar is bare except for a set of candlesticks and a statue of Christ.

Nurse of the Mediterranean

Climb the hill towards the graceful neoclassical, 19th-century **Bighi** complex, once the hospital where the wounded troops of Napoleon and Nelson were treated. Today it houses the Malta Centre of Restoration. During World War I it was known as the 'Nurse of the Mediterranean'. In the Great Siege a Turkish battery operated from **Fort Ricasoli**, on the seaward point across Rinella Creek. The **Rinella Film Facilities Studios** located here and Fort Ricasoli were the location for many of the spectacular scenes in the Ridley Scott film *Gladiator* and the 2004 film *Troy*.

Above: the Inquisitor's Palace, dating from the 16th century, still flies the flags

malta itineraries

5. THE SOUTHEAST *(see map, p10)*

Visit the prehistoric ruins of Borg in-Nadur and Ghar Dalam, the port of Birzebbuga, and the fishing villages of Marsaxlokk and Marsascala. Bring swimming gear and a picnic lunch for Peter's Pool; book ahead to dine at Grabiel in Marsascala.

This 16 km (10-mile) itinerary can be done in one day on foot if you are an enthusiastic walker, but most people will probably prefer to drive.

Approaching **Birzebbuga** from Valletta, look out for the small signpost on the left that points towards the **Ghar Dalam** (Cave of Darkness). If you miss it, make a U-turn at the bottom of the hill. (The bus stops opposite the entrance.) The museum here exhibits fossilised deer, bears, dwarf elephants and hippopotamuses dating back to the Neolithic and Pleistocene eras, but you will find the best relics are in the Museum of Archaeology in Valletta. The discovery of similar fossils in Sicily supports the theory that the islands were once connected, forming a land bridge between Europe and Africa.

   The prehistoric site of **Borg in-Nadur** is also easy to miss; park close to the bus stop at the bottom of the hill, then follow the rocky trail to the ruins. The complex dates from 1400 BC and includes the remains of a megalithic temple, a few bee-hive-shaped stone houses, and a defensive wall.

Gorbachev and Bush

Birzebbuga's charm is almost overwhelmed by the presence of the nearby container ship terminal. Look out for the marker near Kalafrana which commemorates the historic summit meeting convened here by Mikhail Gorbachev and George Bush Snr in December 1989. Just beyond, Pretty Bay is a white sandy beach ringed with attractively painted homes.

Above: a traditional *luzzu* boat at Marsaxlokk
Right: Marsaxlokk's renowned Sunday market

Retrace your steps but at this stage you should keep to the coast road. The picturesque fishing village of **Marsaxlokk** (pronounced *Marsa-shlock*) is ahead on the left. Marsaxlokk is renowned for its Sunday fish market; its daily market mainly sells tourist goods. Walking round the bay you will probably see fishermen cleaning their boats, untangling nets and going about their business as they have for centuries.

Drivers should leave Marsaxlokk via the Valletta road. Walkers should follow the bay, staying well above the power station. Just after the church take a right on Triq San Giuseppe, then another on Triq Melquart. At the roundabout at the top of the hill take the first exit and stay to the left. Some 100 metres (330ft) beyond take a right turn for **Delimara**. At the first fork in the track turn right for Point Delimara. Driving along the crest, you're rewarded with wonderful views of Marsaxlokk and Birzebbuga. Note a sign pointing the way to the car park for **Peter's Pool**.

A Private Swim

The road ends at Fort Delimara, not much further on. For a virtually private swimming pool all to yourself, walk down to **Delimara Bay** to swim; otherwise head for the even quieter **Peter's Pool**. Be careful driving down the track, which is extremely rough. Also be warned that this area is notorious for thieves

who think nothing of breaking your car windows. The best defence is to leave absolutely nothing visible inside.

The path down to the pool is well-trodden. There's no shore, and you can dive into the deep, clear blue water from the rocky shelving. But beware of the currents that swirl under the rocky outcrops at the pool's end. The peninsula seems made for exploring: the paths are conspicuously laid out and there is very little danger of getting lost.

After a picnic and a swim, return to the main road and follow the signs to **St Thomas Bay**. At the next major junction (with Zejtun to the left), turn right for a meandering trip through uninhabited countryside. If on foot, take the more direct path along the shore to St Thomas Bay. Among carpets of wild flowers are salt pans, concealed bays, a communications satellite and the ruins of St Paul's Church. At St Thomas Bay continue around the water or go directly to Marsascala. At the next big intersection, the road turns right and, following the bay, goes past the St Thomas bar and restaurant and the Southern Surfing Club. The club is private, but it rents out sailboards and boats.

A Traditional Fishing Village

The one-way traffic system makes it difficult to get out of St Thomas but eventually signs direct you into the village of **Marsascala**. Unlike many of the fishing villages along the coast, Marsascala has managed to retain its character. Entering the village can be confusing. At the roundabout at the head of the bay, take the right (third) exit then follow the road towards Zonqor Point until signposts direct you into the town centre.

A good choice for dinner – if you don't mind splashing out – is **Grabiel**, a seafood restaurant on the bay that has acquired a devoted following.

6. QUARRIES AND TEMPLES *(see map, p40)*

Visit the Hypogeum and Neolithic temples at Tarxien, and explore one of the stone-working quarries. Enjoy a boat ride through the Blue Grotto and see the historic temples of Hagar Qim and Mnajdra.

A car is essential for this half-day itinerary. If seeing the temples in the morning, maybe take a picnic. Access to the Hypogeum is limited, so book as soon as you arrive in Malta (tel: 2182 5579 or 2180 5021).

The **Hal Saflieni (Hypogeum)** underground burial complex at **Tarxien** has only recently been restored. Following the signs to the airport south of Valletta, take the road to Marsa and travel up the hill – with the Adolorata Cemetery on your right – to the roundabout at the top. Veer right to Tarxien and Paola, where there are signposts to the Hypogeum and Neolithic temples. The subterranean burial place was carved into rocks over a period of hundreds of years between about 2500 BC and 2000 BC with simple tools made from flint and obsidian. The bones of 7,000 people have been found in a burial

chamber that descends several storeys underground. Unfortunately all evidence pertaining to the people who constructed it disappeared mysteriously in about 2000 BC.

Soft Rock

Return to the Tarxien roundabout and follow signs to the airport. Take the road to Kirkop when you reach the main airport roundabout. Pass under a runway and at the next roundabout take a right to Mqabba, passing a large ST Microelectronics plant on your left. As you drive towards **Mqabba**, you will see that the road is lined with quarries, many of them up to 18 metres (60ft) deep, with a maximum working depth of around 24 metres (80ft). Most of Malta's stonework originates here: resembling slabs

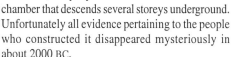

Previous Page: Peter's Pool (top) and Marsaxlokk harbour
Above and **Left:** the prehistoric Hagar Qim temple

of cheddar cheese, the globigerina rock is conveniently soft. After exposure to air, it hardens and changes colour, from yellow to creamy white.

Some of the quarries have been converted into gardens or citrus orchards. One is now the Limestone Heritage, a fascinating quarry open to visitors at Siggiewi (for opening hours call: 2146 4931). Starkly rectangular, the cavities have all been hewn with precision even when done by hand. Modern equipment has of course taken much of the labour, and some of the danger, out of this formerly back-breaking occupation.

Grotto Cruise

Leaving Mqabba, follow the signs for Hagar Qim. Head straight across the first roundabout in the direction of Hagar Qim and Qrendi. After 30 metres (100ft) take an unmarked left turn to **Wied iz-Zurrieq** – the **Blue Grotto** is less than five minutes away. Consisting of several caves and grottoes, it takes its name from the watery reflections of the colourful limestone corals and minerals. From the car park follow signs to the landing stage. The grotto cruise lasts about 30 minutes and is subject to weather conditions. Agree the price before boarding a boat.

After the cruise, you might want to spend some time browsing around the small fishing enclave. There are a number of restaurants, bars, and souvenir handicraft shops here. The clear waters that lie between the Wied and the small island of Filfla provide excellent diving conditions.

A left turn a few hundred metres up the road leads to **Hagar Qim** (Standing Stones), less than 2km (1 mile) away. This prehistoric temple overlooking the sea was constructed with globigerina limestone, and some of the slabs are among the largest in the world. A temple of the Ggantija period, Hajar Qim features carvings which do not appear anywhere else in Malta.

Down the hill, **Mnajdra**, the sister temple, enjoys a beautiful site overlooking the sea. (The **Filfla** island nature reserve opposite was once used by the British army as a firing range.) Dating from 3000 BC to 1500 BC, Mnajdra was built from coralline limestone and consists of three temples, with a common outside wall. Seen from above, the chambers of the middle temple resemble a woman's body. People believed that a fertility goddess's control of the elements ensured a fruitful harvest. The temples were used for sacrificial purposes, and gifts of milk and blood were presented at the altars. Note the square holes in the Oracle chamber, behind which hidden priests spoke to worshippers. This is a good place for a picnic and, in the early evening, for watching the sunset.

Right: carvings above the underground burial complex of Tarxien

7. THE SOUTH COAST *(see map below)*

A day trip taking in Verdala Palace, Buskett Gardens, prehistoric cart tracks and caves at 'Clapham Junction', and a walk along Dingli Cliffs.

This 11 km (7-mile) itinerary is easily walked in a day. In a car it takes less than two hours (plus walking time on cliffs). Another option is to take the bus, though the service is infrequent. Consider bringing a picnic.

Leaving Rabat, the road to Verdala passes St Dominic's Church, after which **Verdala Palace** is less than 2km (1 mile) away on the left. Built in 1586 by Grand Master Hugues Louvenx de Verdale as his summer residence, and later serving as a summer residence for British governors, the palace occupies a commanding position, surrounded by gardens, with views across the island. Designed by Cassar, it has frescoed walls and a graceful, oval staircase. The small **chapel** in the grounds, which is dedicated to St Anthony the Abbot, also dates back to the late 16th century. (Not open to visitors.)

Malta's Only Woods

Buskett Gardens (from the Italian *boschetto* – 'small wood'), Malta's only true wooded area, is a short downhill walk from the palace. In December and January, when they are harvested, the aroma of oranges permeates the air. The snack bar sells drinks and refreshments and the gardens have plenty of popular

Above: above the cliffs at Dingli

The South Coast

1000 m / 1100 yards

- - - **Itinerary 7**

Gnien is-Sultan
Domus Romana
Mdina
St Paul
St Augustine
Nigred
St Agatha's Church & Catacombs
RABAT
Underground Chapel
Tombs
Ta' Laknija
Ta' Dekozzu
Dominican Monastery
Tal-Virtu'
Hofret ir-Rizz
Gnien il-Kbir
Misrah Suffara
Gnien iz-Zghir
Il-Hawlija
Ix-Xaghra ta l-Isqof
Dingli
Verdala Palace
Tal-Pitkal
Buskett Gardens
Tar-Raba'
Dingli Cliffs
Tal-Vecca
Chajn il-Kbiva
Cave Dwellings
Ghar Il-Kbir
Madalene
Inquisitor's Palace
Clapham Junction (Cart Tracks)
Ghar Mundu
Rdum Dikkiena
Ta' Zuta
MEDITERRANEAN SEA
Buxih
Underground Chapel

picnic spots. They are also the site of great activity on the eve of 29 June, when *Mnajra*, the feast of St Peter and St Paul, is celebrated.

Near Buskett, a sign points to **Clapham Junction**, site of prehistoric cart tracks, and caves that were inhabited until the 19th century. At the end of a road which looks like a car park, turn left. A sign near the top of the small hill points to the cart tracks. Park at the end. Some historians suggest that the tracks were established as a specific route, by early man carrying carts, others claim that they are the result of natural erosion. Situated less than 100 metres (about 300ft) along the upper path, the caves are the only ones in the area.

Drive back down the hill and cross the top of the 'car park'. At the first T-junction head right. The road rolls through countryside, eventually passing the **Inquisitor's Palace**, behind an elaborate gate. Visitors are not allowed access as it is used for government purposes. A few minutes later the road rounds a bend and the sea down below comes into view. From here the road leads to **Dingli**, about 3km (2 miles) away, and there are stunning views of the south coast. The cliffs fall sharply to the sea, and it is an ideal place for walking. If you arrived by bus, wait for your return trip outside the **Bobbyland** restaurant.

8. EXPLORING MALTA'S TAIL *(see map, p46)*

A morning or afternoon drive through a sparsely populated area, visiting the Shrine of St Mary of Mellieha, the Red Tower, and Popeye Village. Take a picnic or try Mellieha's Arches Restaurant for lunch.

Start at Pwales Beach, at the head of St Paul's Bay. A car is essential.

As you drive up from the bay, you can't help but notice **Selmun Palace**, an 18th-century affair designed by Domenico Cachia, round the bend near the summit of the first hill. Continue to the roundabout, take the exit marked **Mellieha Centre** and drive through the town. Look out for the Arches Restaurant on the left about 30 metres/100ft before the Our Lady Chapel.

Take the first left around the base of **Mellieha Church** and park at the top of the hill near the cemetery and children's playground. You might want to take a stroll, see the local sights and absorb the atmosphere, after which the nearby **Sea View Café** is a wonderful place for a cold drink, especially in the heat of the morning sun. From the terrace of the small bar, Mellieha Bay is spread out below with the White Tower on Marfa Ridge clearly visible.

St Paul Prayed Here

Walk back to see **Our Lady Chapel**, one of the island's oldest, most venerated ecclesiastical institutions. Not only was it hewn from a rock but, according to the local legend, it was the site of St Paul's prayers after he was shipwrecked not far from the island's coastline. Though the

Right: soaking up the sun

chapel is modest in size, there are, on the upper walls and the roof, some particularly lovely frescoes that date back to the 11th century.

Return to your car and the main road for the drive to Malta's 'tail'. Head left down the hill, past the crescent-shaped, sandy **Il-Ghadira Beach**, one of Malta's largest and most popular. Be warned that the road behind it is invariably crowded in high summer. Climb the hill towards the recently renovated **Red Tower** fortress at the peak. Take a left at the roundabout at the top of the ridge opposite the road marked 'Armier, Little Armier'. The wonderful views from the ridge are unfortunately somewhat marred by electric power lines. If you want to explore the area on foot, take the semi-dirt road past the tower to **Ras il-Qammieh** at the south of the tail.

Fiesta Celebrations

To reach the tail's north end, return to the main road and take the road opposite, which runs along the top of **Marfa Ridge** with Mellieha Bay below on the right. This is a popular summer resort for islanders, and from the cliffs you'll see many anchored boats, their occupants picnicking or swimming off the nearby rocks. Several roads lead the other way off this main route – but none interconnect, so you must retrace your steps to the main road – including the one to Armier, which hosts celebrations after every major *festa*. At **Dahlet ix-Xilep** there's a small statue of the Madonna and a Lady Chapel, from which the **White Tower** is a 15–20 minute walk away.

Return to the main road, and Il-Ghadira, following the signposts to **Popeye Village**, built for the 1981 movie starring Robin Williams. To conclude the itinerary, return the way you came. There are plenty of good picnic spots around here; or you could head straight to Mellieha for lunch at the Arches. If you are in the mood to participate in (or watch) any of a variety of water sports, the well-signposted **Golden Bay** is a five-minute drive away.

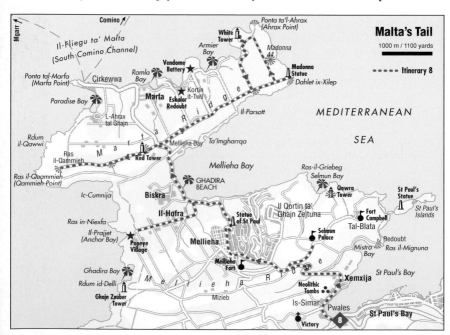

9. A NIGHT ON THE TOWN *(see pullout map)*

There are lots of nightlife options in Paceville, Bugibba and Qawra, and Marsascala. Nightlife in Gozo focuses on Marsalforn and Xlendi, but mostly in summer. This itinerary looks at the bars, discos, clubs, casinos and a range of eateries featuring cuisine from all over the world.

The Maltese love to party. During most summer nights and at weekends throughout the year, traffic in the main areas is intense: you can spend more time looking for parking than wining and dining. **Paceville**, a mecca for Maltese youngsters and visitors in search of exciting nightlife, pulsates with all kinds of music from early evening to the following morning.

You should be sure to pick your dining spot early: **Spinola Bay** is ideal for a quiet start to the night at San Giuliano or La Dolce Vita for fresh fish and continental cuisine. Or you might try The Blue Elephant Thai restaurant in the Hilton complex, or the Greek-style Bouzouki. There are pasta and pizza joints aplenty – The Avenue is one of the most popular – and international franchises such as Henry J Bean's. Maltese nights start at about midnight, after which you will have to jostle to reach the bar at venues such as Il Fuego (Latin and salsa dance music), The Alley, Bamboo Bar, Footloose, The Havana Club, Coconut Grove, the Axis Disco and Hacienda. For a quieter evening you might start with a sumptuous meal at Barracuda along the **Balluta** seafront. You might try The Dragonara casino (near the Westin Dragonara Hotel, St Julian's) for a flutter on the slot machines, roulette, blackjack or chemin de fer.

Family Entertainment

The **Bay Street Complex** has a number of affordable restaurants. Within walking distance is a cinema complex (including a giant Imax screen), a Superbowl, and the Cynergi Fitness Centre.

The **St Paul's Bay/Bugibba/Qawra** locality is geared towards family entertainment, with lots of restaurants and

Above: one reason why Paceville is a mecca for youngsters
Right: try your luck at The Dragonara casino's roulette wheel

bars around Pioneer Road and Bay Square. Maltese families party here at weekends – the presence of children is tolerated into the small hours.

La Stalla is a popular pasta and pizza joint opposite the more refined Da Michele on the Triq it-Turisti road. The choice of dining options includes The China Palace, Gopal's Indian Restaurant and the Italian-style Ristorante Gran Laguna. Try a typical Maltese dish of fried rabbit with chips at the Bigfoot Bar and Restaurant, or mouthwatering choice cuts at the Argentinian Steak House next to the Empire Cinema complex.

The **Dolmen Resort Hotel** offers The Oracle casino, the Amazonia night-club, the refined La Sybille restaurant, and Batubulan Lido.

Bands play at a number of venues, including O'Connors and most hotels in summer. Paceville's popular Il Fuego has also branched out to Qawra, where the salsa and disco bars around Bay Square are busy through the night.

Mecca for the Young

Marsascala has been transformed in recent years. Now attracting patrons from the south side of the island who want to avoid the hustle and bustle of Paceville and Bugibba, it has loads of new restaurants and bars. Many such places offer free snacks – *escargots*, fresh sea urchins and *bigilla*, a broad-bean paste. Marsascala's La Favorita restaurant in Triq il-Gardiel serves fresh fish and a variety of other Maltese dishes. Grabiel, Jakarta, Awwista and the Red Lobster are also recommended.

If you are feeling adventurous, you could start the evening with a splendid meal at La Favorita in Marsascala and then drive to Vittoriosa for a late-night fling at the Casino di Venezia on the Vittoriosa waterfront. Or dine at Il Medina or the gloriously refurbished Xara Palace in Mdina and then drive the short distance to the Gianpula disco in the outskirts of Rabat, or to the Numero Uno disco at Ta' Qali. The Corinthia Palace Hotel at Attard (near San Anton Gardens) hosts The Rickshaw, which does Indonesian, Malaysian, Thai, Indian, Singaporean and Chinese dishes.

If you really want to push the boat out on a weekend summer evening, dine at the splendid Arches Restaurant *(see Itinerary 8, page 45)* in Mellieha, drive the short distance to Cirkewwa, then board the all-night ferry to Gozo. Once there, drive off to Xlendi and the La Grotta disco and you probably won't be fit or willing to return to your base until the early hours of the morning.

When holidaying in **Gozo**, the Stone Crab restaurant on the Xlendi Bay waterfront offers a selection of fish and pizza. La Grotta disco is a short walking distance away if you have accommodation in Xlendi.

A final word about driving in Malta and Gozo – traffic is heavy and erratic. Breathalyser tests (EU standards) are statutory. Parking can always be a problem – day and night, wardens are frequently on the prowl, and clamping and towing are accompanied by hefty fines.

Above: for a relaxing start to the evening, try San Giuliano restaurant in Spinola Bay

Gozo
Itineraries

Gozo is said to be the island where, in Homer's *Odyssey*, the nymph Calypso kept Odysseus captive for seven years. Standing atop one of the many terraced hills you can see why Odysseus made no attempt to escape; many modern visitors never want to leave either.

The history of Gozo has been inextricably linked with that of Malta, its larger island neighbour to the southeast. During the Phoenician and Roman periods, however, Gozo was treated as an independent country, called Gwl then Gaulus. Saracen Arabs ruled both islands, during which time Gozo remained largely Christian. The legacy of Spanish rule was the name Gozo (Joy in Spanish). The Arabic name Ghawdex (pronounced *Owdesh*) returned in the 16th century, and this is how Gozitans refer to their island today.

The Knights of St John treated Malta and Gozo equally. But Gozo had none of Malta's natural defences, and was thus particularly vulnerable to both piracy and foreign invasion. In 1551 there was precious little protection against marauding Ottomans who ransacked the island. Gozo had a short period of independence (1798–1800) when Malta was ruled by the French. Under the British, Malta and Gozo were united. Gozo has its own bishop and cathedral, and has been an independent diocese since 1864.

A third of the size of Malta, Gozo is 14km (9 miles) long and, at its broadest point, 6km (4 miles) wide. Though its shoreline measures only 137km (85 miles) it is rarely crowded apart from the areas around Marsalforn and Xlendi in July and August. The ferry crossing from Malta takes 25 - minutes, but, for such a short distance, the contrast between the islands is marked: the northwestern end of Malta is rocky and barren, whereas Gozo's ferry harbour is surrounded by lush vegetation. In the hinterland behind the harbour, gently terraced fields climb flat-topped hills, many crowned with villages built as defensive outposts at a time when foreign invasion was a dire threat.

Living by the Elements

Fishing and farming were the primary sources of income on Gozo, but tourism is now making its mark. With a landmass of 67 sq km (26 sq miles), and a population of 25,000, Gozo adheres to the solid values of those who live by the elements. Horse-drawn carts are as common as tractors, and it is quite possible to walk for an hour or more along country lanes and goat tracks without seeing another soul, save a farmer hoeing his fields or a young shepherd tending goats or sheep.

Right: the quaint harbour at Mgarr

10. THE ISLAND'S HISTORICAL CORE *(see map below)*

Explore the capital, Victoria (known often to locals as Rabat, its older name), lunch on local specialities at Oleander or Gesthers, in Xaghra, and visit Ggantija prehistoric temple. Finish at Gozo Heritage.

A day trip from Malta, spending half a day in Victoria. You can travel on Gozo's buses: confirm departure times and change en route to Gozo Heritage.

If driving, there is parking in **Victoria** behind the bus depot but most spaces are gone by 9.30am. You could breakfast at any cafe here – the service is good, the food home-made. The Book Rose on Republic Street sells English-language newspapers.

There are, in close proximity, a **tourist office** at the corner of Palm Street, a post office and the Astra Theatre. At **Pjazza Indipendenza** (known locally as **It Tokk**) is a World War II memorial. The other monumental building is the **Banca Giuratale**, erected in 1733 by Grand Master Vilhena. The **Café Jubilee** here serves a great cappuccino. To enter the labyrinth that constitutes Victoria's oldest part (**Il Borgo**), take the short street by **Gangu's Bar** (a favourite with the locals, as is the nearby **Ginevra**). During the week the street hosts a small vegetable market. **St George's Square** is at the end, and the eye is drawn to the magnificent facade of the baroque church of the same name. Built in 1678, in the shape of a cross, it is a seamless mixture of old and new. The altar, installed in 1967, is a copy of one which Bernini carved for St Peter's in Rome. The canopy over the altar features a gilded angel at each corner; ornate carved pillars surround the side altars.

Gozo Green

To the right of the church, St George Street describes a winding, meandering route lined by small shops and old houses. Note the balconies and the doors painted in a shade known as Gozo green. At the first T-junction, take a right and an almost immediate left. At a junction with a statue of St George on the corner building, go left, and the street shortly opens on to **Piazza Santu Wistin**. The south side of the square is terraced with two-storey, Gozitan residences, each with an enclosed balcony above the central door. At the far end of the square, the 19th-century **Church of St Augustine** is flanked by four statues.

Return the way you came. Take a right on **Triq Il-Karita**, then a left at the first T-junction up School Street. Next you come to a particularly timeless part of Victoria. Look for a statue of the Madonna

and a Child accepting bread rolls from a kneeling supplicant, then go right. This is **Narrow Street**, a long courtyard where women work on their lace patterns and children play. Ignore the electric wires running overhead, and you could be in another century.

Hakim's Home, Bishop's Palace

Return to the street from which you came, and turn right. The road opposite St James's Church leads straight up to the **citadel**; climb to the tree-shaded terrace opposite for a view of the massive fortifications and the cathedral. In the citadel's **Piazza Katidral** are three main buildings: the cathedral takes centre stage; on its left, in the 17th-century **Palace of the Governors** are the law courts; the right side is given over to the **Chapter Hall**, which dates back to 1899, and the **Bishop's Palace** which, until 1551, was a residence of the *hakim* (Muslim governor) of Gozo.

The Church of the Assumption, better known as the **cathedral** and designed by Lorenzo Gafa, was built between 1697 and 1711 on the site of a temple dedicated to Juno. It is best known for its interior with a *trompe l'oeil* dome. Painted by Antonio Manuele Poggo in 1739, it gives the appearance of being a dome, but the ceiling is actually flat.

Before taking a walk around the bastions, you might want to spend some time in the citadel's five small museums (all open Monday to Saturday 8.30am–4.30pm, Sunday till 3pm). The **Folklore Museum** off Triq Il-Fosse is situated in three 16th-century houses which are as interesting as the excellent exhibits. The **Cathedral Museum**, further up Il-Fosse, has some of the columns from the Juno temple. Back in the square, the **Armoury** and **Natural Science Museums** are opposite each other on Quarters Street, beyond the house with the shrine to Ta'Pinu. The **Archaeology Museum** (through

Above: the citadel, featuring five small museums
Right: the cathedral, built without a dome

the small arch to the right of the cathedral square in Palazzo Bondi) has a great range of relics, from prehistoric Gozo through Punic, Roman, Byzantine and Arabic eras, to medieval tombstones.

Former cells on Prison Street host a **Crafts Centre** and **Lace Workshop**, from where a stairwell leads to **St Michael's Bastion**. Walk in a clockwise direction; a set of steps leads to a walkway across the top of the citadel's entrance, with the best views of the piazza.

To continue along the bastions, climb the steps to **St Martin's Cavalier**; to the right are the ruins of buildings destroyed in the earthquake of 1693. The walkway starts to curve and the wall blocks the view, until you reach the telescope. Here you can look out for the Cross of St Joseph with glimpses of Marsalforn, the fishing village and popular beach resort, in the distance behind it.

Take the long flight of steps down to the rear of the citadel. Here the walls' thickness can best be appreciated. You can make a circuit through the lower part, walking the narrow streets edged by high walls and ruins. When it comes to lunch, try a snack at **Ta' Ricardo** on Bastion Street. Only local produce is used including cheeses, sun-dried tomatoes and Ricardo's own wine. Or drive to **Xaghra**. **Gesther's** (open from noon), on the main street near the square, is good for local fare. Or, in the square, try the trendy but casual **Oleander**.

A Female Giant

The temple of **Ggantija** (Female Giant) probably dates from 3600 BC–3000 BC and is one of the oldest free-standing stone buildings discovered. There are two temples, each with its own entrance but sharing a circular forecourt. Some parts of the perimeter walls, which rise to 6 metres (20ft), contain megalithic stones weighing up to 45,000kg (50 tons). The myth says the female giant Sansuna carried the stones from Ta'Cenc on her head.

To reach Gozo Heritage by bus, ask the driver to let you off at the Mgarr/Victoria road. Within 20 minutes another bus, heading to Mgarr/Malta Ferry, should arrive. If you are driving, follow signposts to Mgarr/Malta Ferry; **Gozo Heritage** (Open Monday to Saturday 8.30am–4.30pm, Sunday till 3pm) is on the left a little way beyond St Cecilia's Tower. Situated in a renovated farmhouse, the centre's exhibits cover the 6,000 years of Gozitan history, from Stone Age cavemen to modern independence. From here, the drive to the jetty – from where you can catch a ferry to Malta – takes five minutes.

Above: the bastions command fine views
Right: the 5,000-year-old temple of Ggantija

11. A RING AROUND THE ISLAND   *(see map, p54)*

A full day's circumnavigation of Gozo, by car, taking in Nadur, Dahlet Qorrot, Ramla Bay, Calypso's Cave, Marsalforn, the Salt Pans, Zebbug, Gharb, the shrine of Ta'Pinu, Fungus Rock, the Azure Window, Xlendi, Mgarr Ix-Xini, and the domed church of Xewkija.

This itinerary is designed to avoid Victoria, but head for it if you get lost.

Leaving the ferry harbour, take the road to **Nadur**. Driving towards the town, you will notice the windmills to your right, in Qala. These are among the last remaining windmills of the many that once dotted the countryside.

The church of **SS Peter and Paul**, built in 1760, dominates Nadur's main square. Drive north from the church square and at Triq Dicembru 13 take a left. Turn left again at the first T-junction, then right at the following T-junction. Look for signs to **San Blas Bay** and **Dahlet Qorrot**. At the first fork, go left to San Blas Bay if you feel like undertaking an extremely steep, 185-metre (600 ft) walk from the parking area to the water. For the easier option, take the right turn to the old fishing harbour of Dahlet Qorrot. There are concrete steps that lead to the upper cliff, where you can walk. Alternatively, you might try the more precarious lower path at the water's edge.

Once you have finished walking, take the road back to Nadur, but at the first T-junction go right towards Ramla. At the second T-junction head towards Victoria, and at the next junction follow the sign to Ramla once again. Halfway down the road you should find a small lookout site with views of the valley. The terraced fields are filled with fig and orange trees. Screens made from local bamboo protect the crops from the wind.

The Best Beach

Ramla Bay is Gozo's longest and best beach. In the summer, stake out an early claim to be assured of space. The short cut to **Calypso's Cave** (avoiding Xaghra) is easily missed: about 30 metres (100ft) beyond the small police station, a steep, single-lane, gravel road bears to the right. If the short cut looks too daunting, follow the signs to Xaghra, where directions to Calypso's Cave are clearly posted. The cave is not much more than a narrow, rocky slit where the Siren allegedly kept Odysseus captive for seven years, but the views of Ramla Bay are excellent.

When you leave, take the main road to Xaghra, and at the first T-junction go right. The road to **Marsalforn** is well-marked. Teeming with life in the summer, the village is popular with locals and tourists alike. Swimmers have a choice of rock, shingle and sand beaches. Even at the height of the season in July and August, it is worth braving the crowds to lunch at **Otters**, a family-run establishment

Right: one of the island's last remaining windmills

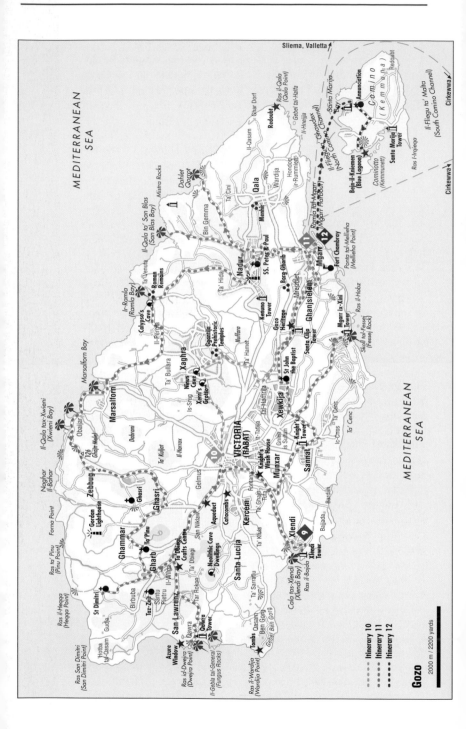

Gozo

Itinerary 10
Itinerary 11
Itinerary 12

2000 m / 2200 yards

on the water's edge. Fishing is still a major industry in Marsalforn and the catch is brought in every day and sold, often straight from the boats, from the harbour area in front of the **Calypso Hotel**.

To reach the **Salt Pans**, follow the road that runs parallel to Marsalforn's waterfront. Take the first right turn; just before the quay, a road swings left up the hill leading to the upper promenade where older houses are located. In the bay beyond the locally popular **Qbajjar Restaurant**, follow the road as it leads under a sandstone cliff (water will lap at the wheels of your vehicle), and around the next bend are the salt pans – shallow pools cut from the soft coastal rock. Although Gozo now imports all the salt it needs, many people still collect it here each September.

The Best View

Return to the start of the pans and, beyond the overhang, a right turn leads to **Zebbug**. This attractive village occupies the top of a ridge and offers wonderful views of the island. After a climb in first gear, the first flat area is the church-fronted main square. For the best view over the island, leave as though heading for Victoria, but shortly after the road forks left take an immediate right, followed by a left.

Continuing past a school, the road leads to a rest stop with benches and a car park. To avoid Victoria, drive down the hill at the far end of the viewing area, and at the cemetery take the gravel road which branches off to the right. It's not signposted, but eventually you will arrive in **Ghasri**. The road at the right of the church runs through **Ghammar** to the shrine church of **Ta'Pinu**. The route you have just taken is off the track beaten by tourists. This is old Gozo, where farmhouses have not been prettified for tourist consumption.

Ta'Pinu church was built between 1920 and 1936, but there has been a chapel here since the 16th century. In the late 19th century a sick woman was believed to have been cured after her son heard a voice in the chapel, since when many believers have come to the church to ask for Our Lady of

Top: a fisherman at Marsalforn tends to his traps
Right: Ta'Pinu church, constructed in the first half of the 20th century

Ta'Pinu's intercession. A room to the right of the Lady Chapel is filled with discarded crutches and leg braces, baby clothes and newspaper clippings telling of miracles attributed to Ta'Pinu. At the conclusion of many Gozitan weddings, the bride places her bouquet on the altar of the **Lady Chapel** in the hope of securing a happy marriage.

Leaving Ta'Pinu, take the road to Victoria, then turn left at the **Gharb** sign. As you enter the town, keep an eye open for the controversial church facade: some believe that this 17th-century architectural gem is nothing more than a copy of Francesco Borromini's Sant'Agnes on Rome's Piazza Navona, others claim that it is original. Either way, the exterior is a delight. Inside, the church is smaller than expected, but it's a splendidly ornate baroque structure. In the square, the **Market Cross** is one of the finest on the island. You might be in the square when, heralded by a distinctive chime, the market van, selling fruit, vegetables, chickens and rabbits, rolls into town.

San Dimitri's Lantern

Drive through Gharb and take the narrow road to **San Dimitri** with its small chapel. This typical stretch of Gozitan countryside leads to a rock escarpment and a coast that looks towards Sicily. Legend has it that in the 16th century invading Turks kidnapped a Gozitan youth. After his mother prayed to San Dimitri for his return, the youth was whisked off the Turkish galley and back to land. On stormy nights, San Dimitri's lantern is said to glow in the sea, as it did when the saint guided the boy back to shore. On the road back to Gharb, look out for **il-Fanal ta' Giordano**, a lighthouse whose panning beacon can be seen from Malta's north coast at night.

When the road from Gharb turns right near San Lawrenz en route to Dwejra, look out for the landmark **Gozo Glass-blowing Centre**. A short distance

further on is the **Ta'Dbiegi Crafts Village** which is easy to miss. Although this centre features some excellent pottery, it is really nothing more than a glorified series of souvenir shops.

Before heading for the village of **San Lawrenz**, look out for the **Kempinski San Lawrenz Leisure Resort** on your left. This, Gozo's latest five-star hotel, is situated in a beautiful Maltese stone building set at the bottom of a valley. One of the hotel's interest-

Top: the Gharb church's disputed facade
Above: lace-makers, Fontana Cottage Industry

ing features is the descent from the lobby, not only to the bedrooms but also to a splendid array of palm trees and swimming pools.

As you drive downhill to **Dwejra Bay**, Wied Ilma is to the left, and beyond it, the scars of the sandstone quarries. Stop near **Qawra Tower**, which you can climb for sweeping views of the bay. To the extreme left you will see the **Fungus Rocks**. The plant that grew on these rocks was reputed to have miraculous healing powers. To the right is the **Azure Window**, whose arch is a natural feature carved out of the rock by the constant pounding of water. Similarly, the paths and walkways near the shoreline change every year as the result of wind and sea erosion. The rocks are sharp and often slippery so caution is urged, as is the use of good shoes with non-slip soles. If you decide to swim off the rocks, be sure to wear rubber or plastic shoes.

Fertile Ground for Fossil-Hunters

Take a few minutes to check out the fossil-rich coastal terrain to the left of the little church. Although many of the fossils have been chipped away by collectors and curio seekers, some classic examples remain. These include the fossilised bones of a large sea serpent, which are clearly etched into the rocks. To climb the Azure Window, take the path behind the church. Divers love exploring these rocks. You might pay one of the local boatmen to take you for a sightseeing excursion through the **Inland Sea** pool.

To get to **Xlendi**, you cannot avoid Victoria, but at least you can bypass the centre, and the route is well signposted. On Victoria's Xlendi side, on Triq Tal-ghajn you will come to Fontana Cottage Industry with its workforce of lace-makers. Opposite is a 17th-century **wash house**. Both make for interesting stops. From here, Xlendi is about 2km (1 mile) away. Park behind the row of buildings that fronts the bay, or take the road on the left up towards the apartment complexes and park at the top of the bluff. The hillside has been landscaped down to the water, each level connected by steps and walkways. Swimming from the rocks is popular and you might see divers preparing for underwater explorations.

A concrete path leads back along an inlet of the bay. Cross the small bridge and walk to the **tower** on **Ras Il-Bajda**. The sandstone here is smooth enough for comfortable sunbathing and, although some of the rocks near the bay's entrance are sharp, the swimming is generally good. The cliffs of Gebel Ben Gorg and Wardija Point stretch towards the northwestern horizon. Heading in the other direction, you might enjoy a seaside walk for several hundred metres before the path ends at the water's edge. Ambitious walkers can hike all the way along the clifftops to **Ta'Cenc**.

Next on this circular tour is a long sliver of water, **Mgarr Ix-Xini**, an

Right: the Azure Window, carved out of the rock by relentless water erosion

ancient port once used by sailors in longboats and galleys for repairs and rest. To bypass Victoria, retrace your route from Xlendi as far as a concrete bus shelter, where an extremely sharp right, signed **Munxar**, takes you through that town and toward **Sannat**. Once there, take the road that swings round the left of the church. Within a minute or so, a green-edged sign points left to Mgarr Ix-Xini. Where the hill is at its lowest, a single-lane road veers to the right. The small fishing harbour is well off the tourist track.

To get to the domed church of St John the Baptist in **Xewkija**, return to the main road, take a right and at the next T-junction turn right again (Mgarr is signposted). This road leads to the church – a modern building of staggering dimensions. The 75-metre (246-ft) high dome, with a circumference of 85 metres (279ft), is one of the four largest in Europe. The remains of the original church, dating from 1665, are through a door on the left of the main altar.

To get the Malta ferry, return to the main road, following signs to Mgarr.

12. Cruise to Comino *(see map, p54)*

Take a boat to Comino and swim in the clear waters of the Blue Lagoon.

Either embark on a ferry from Mgarr, or take a half- or a full-day trip with a pleasure cruise company from one of the island's other ports.

The 2nd-century Greek writer Ptolemy referred to the tiny island of **Comino**, situated between Malta and Gozo, as Cosyra. The name Comino derives from the cumin spice that grows wild here. Although the islanders no longer cultivate cumin in large quantities, it still grows wild in clumps throughout the island. But it is the pink and mauve wild thyme that assails the visitor's eyes and nose, especially in spring, when the bees produce what some claim to be the region's finest honey. The island is only 5 sq km (2 sq miles) in area and is virtually uninhabited – until fairly recently there were only three full-time residents. Comino commands breathtaking views of the two larger islands. It used to be a notorious haven for the pirates who raided the sea traffic between Malta and Gozo up until the time of the Knights.

As you sail towards the island, the first noteworthy sight is the **Santa Marija Tower**. Constructed by the Knights in 1618 as a defence against

the ever-present threat of an Ottoman invasion, it was one of a series of coastal towers that can still be found in Malta and Gozo. As it turned out, the Turks did not launch an attack so the tower was never put to the test. The Santa Marija Tower, currently being restored, now serves as a post for Malta's modest armed forces.

A Perfect Day

For a perfect day, sail around the island's imposing cliffs, anchor in one of the many tiny coves and spend the day swimming and

Left: Santa Marija Tower, built by the Knights

diving in the clear blue water. On the island itself there are no cars, or even roads, only footpaths. Since 1964 (the year of Malta's independence), however, Comino has enjoyed something of a tourist boom, though it is too small to become a real victim of mass-market package tours. The water-sports centre was expanded to include a surf area with qualified instructors, a fine diving base and a diving school.

Amenities for Day Trippers

Out of earshot of the visiting hordes, the **Comino Hotel** (closed for refurbishment) offers many amenities, even for day trippers. It does a good buffet lunch by the pool and is a venue for sea sports such as diving, sailing and jet-skiing. It also has professional tennis tutors, and a separate block of 45 apartments.

If you want to go ashore for a walk, the main landing point is **Santa Marija Bay**. You will find the small **Church of the Annunciation** near the bay, and along the path to the tower are the remains of a Knights' quarantine hospital. There are two sandy beaches, the larger at Santa Marija Bay, but you are bound to be tempted by a swim in the inviting waters of the **Blue Lagoon**, between the main island and Cominotto, a rocky offshore islet.

This is the Mediterranean at its very best. The water's colour ranges from indigo to turquoise and even the dolphins that playfully bob up and down in the deep-sea channels between the islands seem to appreciate the location. You can snorkel and swim here in some of the Mediterranean's clearest waters. But be warned: Maltese and Gozitan people also recognise the beauty of this place, and it can get very crowded.

Top: the Blue Lagoon represents the Mediterranean at its best
Right: posing on Comino

Excursions

I f you have enough time in your schedule you can take advantage of the
various enjoyable tours and excursions available on the island. This is
a good idea because such trips are difficult to organise on your own.
Sea tours usually start from The Strand in Sliema or the quay at Bugibba
– most hotels will have details and schedules. Moreover, wherever you
go you are likely to be offered leaflets and literature on the available options. Due to Malta's geographical proximity to Sicily, and also the grow-
ing speed of communications, there has been an increase in one- and
two-day visits to Sicily, which is less than 100km (62 miles) away. Or
you might decide on a similar two-day cruise to Tunisia, which is 290km
(180 miles) away.

SHORT-TERM CRUISES

Two-day excursions at reasonable prices that include accommodation and
full board on a cruise ship sail weekly from Malta. Travel agents on the
island will have details. The price will often include discounts for children.
There are also longer cruises to Italy's western coast that visit the Bay of
Naples, the holiday resort of Sorrento and the ruins of the ancient Roman city
of Pompeii.

CRUISE THE MALTESE ARCHIPELAGO – DAY OR NIGHT

No visit to Malta and Gozo can be complete without a day-long cruise around
the Maltese archipelago. Daily sailings (weather permitting) normally depart
from The Strand in Sliema. The main operator is Captain Morgan Cruises
(tel: 2134 3373; fax: 2133 2004; e-mail: info@captainmorgan.com.mt),
whose fleet of 21 vessels includes the splendid yacht *Fernandes*, which specialises in late night cruises. There are, in addition, options for motorboat and
sailing boat cruises.

On day tours to Comino and Gozo,
the boat sails in a clockwise direction, cruising eastward through the
open sea into the harbour at
Marsaxlokk, then south and west past
The Blue Grotto and Filfla, under
Dingli Cliffs and past Golden and
Anchor Bays to Comino. Lunch is
served after you have had the opportunity to take a swim in the sur-
rounding waters or a quick wander
around Comino. Later the cruise con-

Left and Right: take to the water

tinues to the north coast of Gozo past Ramla Bay and Marsalforn, then onto Dwejra Bay with its Azure Window and Fungus Rock, past Xlendi, and under the sheer cliffs at Ta' Cenc. The cruise then returns through the Gozo Channel and passes Malta's northern coastline via Mellieha, St Paul's Bay, along St Julian's and back to Sliema.

Besides Captain Morgan Cruises, tours are also organised by Hera Tours (tel: 2134 7483), Oki-Ko-Ki Banis (tel: 2133 9831) and a number of other operators. These companies also do night cruises that stop at a bay (usually Comino) for a barbecue and then a disco party. Some operators also offer a more sedate and romantic evening trip with dinner and views of the Grand Harbour lights by night, the wonders of the floodlit Valletta and Cottonera Bastions.

FISHING TRIPS

This part of the Mediterranean is excellent for angling enthusiasts. A number of fishing-tour organisers run trips that go as far as the island of Panteleria to the east of Malta. The companies provide tackle and bait, guidance on the best fishing areas, and food and drink. Two of the most reputable ones are: Pirotta Fishing Centre (tel: 2133 1279; fax: 2132 2712), which organises daily trips, and Mister Fish (tel: 2142 1418/2167 6244). The catch may vary but it is mostly typically Mediterranean – bream, sea bass, grouper, the much-loved Maltese *lampuka* (dolphin fish) and tuna.

AN UNDERWATER SAFARI

For a leisurely subterranean adventure, take a 90-minute cruise that casts off from the Bugibba quay in St Paul's Bay. Seated in a specially designed glass-bottom boat, passengers can scrutinise the marine life below while the boat makes its journey. The boat's specialist guide will point out and identify each species to you as it darts past the boat. Even if your knowledge of the underwater world is only goldfish-deep when you set out, you will finish the tour feeling like an expert.

ON THE ROAD

For all its advantages, driving in Malta can be a major hassle, so it is just as well that numerous local tour operators – such as Drifter Mini Buses and Tours (tel: 2152 3535) and C Lion Travel (tel:

Above: fishing for all ages
Right: a 1920s bus visits the Three Cities

2157 2706) – are more than willing to relieve you of dependence on a vehicle. Summer nights are an especially good time to be free of responsibility for a car. From July to mid-September, the nights are dedicated to *festa* (fiesta) celebrations, with particularly intense party activities taking place at weekends. These include mass band marches, sightseeing and firework displays. If getting to the fiesta might give you a headache, trying to park could bring on a migraine. For the most relaxing option, join one of the minibus or coach tours organised by the majority of hotels and localities.

A number of companies do Jeep tours to Malta's bays, and trips to Gozo. A quaint 1920 bus tour departs from The Strand, Sliema and takes you to the Three Cities, via a number of fascinating localities, including the Malta dry docks and various points of interest along the Cottonera bastions.

In the course of the journey, the bus travels along the Sliema seafront to Gzira and Manoel Island, to Ta'Xbiex and Msida with their yacht marinas, and on past the Anglican Cemetary (Ta'Braxia) on the right of the road to Porte des Bombes and Blata l-Bajda. From there the bus crosses into Marsa, goes up the hill alongside Malta Shipbuilding, passes the Mosque at Corradino and then into Cospicua.

Down to the Seabed, and up to the Hills

Malta has more than 40 registered and licensed diving schools and centres for what is regarded as the best scuba diving in the Mediterranean region, catering for experts and novices alike. Strict monitoring by the government has ensured that the general safety record is excellent. Sea temperatures usually hit 27°C (80°F) in summer; in winter they rarely drop below 15°C (59°F). All tuition and diving licensing is of international standards. If you are feeling adventurous, try Malta Outdoors Activity Organisers (tel and fax: 2158 4419), which arranges abseiling, climbing, sea kayaking, camping, mountain biking and trekking trips. The company also rents out tents, even though camping facilities are almost non-existent in Malta.

Above: a range of options, from fireworks to folk dancing

Leisure *Activities*

SHOPPING

Malta and Gozo are not known for their shopping. Valletta is the main retail centre. If you are interested in jewellery, the small side streets between Republic Street and Merchants' Street are the place to go. The Savoy Shopping Centre on Republic Street offers a good range of clothes shops, mainly for young people. There are a number of bookshops offering a good selection of books on Maltese topics as well as recent paperbacks from Britain and literature in foreign languages.

With a modicum of luck you can find some superb craft products, such as lace, blown glass, ceramics, silver filigree work, woven goods and knitwear. Lace-making, the island's most traditional craft, dates back to the 16th century. In the 18th century lace items from Malta and Gozo were ordered by aristocrats from all over Europe.

Today, very few local women have the time or inclination to take up this exacting, traditionally female craft, though you can see examples of what is still produced at some of the craft villages on Malta and Gozo listed below. Numerous places advertise 'lace-makers at work', but when you arrive you may be told that 'it's their day off'. Try to buy smaller pieces, which are usually works of finer quality. Typical lace products include tablecloths, napkins, place mats, collars, shawls and delicate blouses.

Blown glass is another speciality. You can watch it being made at locations on Malta and Gozo and then buy the finished product.

Items fashioned from brass and wrought iron, such as door knockers, are beautiful but heavy souvenirs. Door knockers come in various sizes and forms, and are often in the shape of animals or mythical creatures. Very kitschy (and not very practical to carry home) are models of knights made of sheet metal.

Locally made wooden pipes also make for interesting souvenirs. They are made from the trees that grow among heather found on the west of the island. The famous torpedo-shaped Maltese pipes are often decorated with grotesque motifs.

If interested, you ought to visit the pipe factory in Marsa (Carrick Street; open winter: 9am–4pm, summer: 9am–1.30pm). The factory, which dates back to 1930, is owned by one of Malta's oldest companies. Connoisseurs also set great store by the island's tobacco and cigars.

Unfortunately some of the craft centres listed below are increasingly stocking run-of-the-mill souvenir items, and are no longer places where the old island crafts are taught to younger people. However, unless in the course of your travels you run into someone tatting lace or slaving over a potter's wheel, these centres remain the best opportunity to see the local craftspeople at work.

Craft Centres
Ta'Qali Crafts Village
Off Valletta-Rabat Road beyond San Anton Gardens, Attard, Malta.
Tel: 2141 5786; fax: 2141 5787
Open daily 9am–dusk.
This, the largest craft centre on the islands, hosts 15–20 companies on the site of a World War II airfield. Pottery, silver filigree work, glass-blowing, replica knights, weaving and knitting are among the crafts demonstrated. The famous Mdina Glass produced here includes some exquisite products.

Left: market day in Valletta
Right: glass-blowing

Malta Crafts Centre
St John's Square, opp the cathedral, Valletta
Tel: 2124 4532.
Open mid-June–end Sept: Mon–Fri 9am–12.30pm; Oct–mid-June: Mon–Fri 9am–12.30pm and 3–5pm.
This, the Maltese government craft centre, exhibits and sells locally produced arts and crafts. It's also possible to obtain the addresses of craftsmen here.

Mdina Glass
Ta'Qali Crafts Village, Malta
Tel: 2141 5786.
www.mdinaglass.net
Open Mon–Fri 9am–4pm, Sat 9am–noon.
If you enjoy watching glass being blown, this is the place for you. You can buy beautiful hand made souvenirs here – vases, paperweights, etc. The dazzling display is well worth viewing. Gozo Glass at Gharb is another good option.

Ta'Dbiegi Crafts Village
On the road to Dwejra beyond St Lawrence, Gozo
Tel: 2156 1974; fax: 2156 0354
Located in a former barracks, Ta'Dbiegi produces – and sells – items made of leather, wool, ceramics, glass, lace and silver.

Gozo Crafts Centre & Lace-Making Workshop
The Citadel, Victoria
This crafts centre offers a good selection of arts and crafts produced on Gozo.

Gozo Glass
At the 'V' where the Dwejra/San Lawrenz road divides
Tel: 2156 1974; fax: 2156 0354
Hand-made Gozo glass is typically slightly milky with a harmonious mix of colours.

Fontana Cottage Industry
On the Xlendi road, opp the old wash house
You can watch lace-makers at work here. In addition to lace, the souvenir shop also sells knitwear and woven products.

Open Air Markets
Valletta: Mon–Sat until noon on Merchants' Street by St John's Square. Textiles, souvenirs, electronics, etc. Many of the products are cheap imports from Asia.

The Sunday market just outside City Gate, by the bus station in St James's Ditch, is much bigger than the weekday market. It has a flea market and lots of antiquities stalls. The atmosphere is especially pleasant in the early morning.
Cospicua: Tuesday morning. This colourful market is good for clothes, food, household goods, etc.
Marsaxlokk: Mon–Sat until noon, around the waterfront. This market is mainly for tourists. Sunday is the day when local people shop for freshly caught fish.
Rabat: Mon–Sat and Sun until noon. Lots of everything.
Victoria, Gozo: This Sunday morning market on Independence Square is a mecca for visitors and residents alike.

Above: curios, knick-knacks and groceries, all in one small, characterful shop

sport

SPORT

Malta provides facilities for, and is full of fans of, all sorts of sporting activities. As a legacy of the island's British associations, football, rugby union, cricket and horse-racing hold prominent positions in the affections of the populace. Other sports that feature prominently include basketball, athletics, golf, volleyball, karate and judo. Naturally, given the all-pervasive influence of the sea, water sports take pride of place.

Diving

There are 40 licensed diving schools in Malta and Gozo, and diving and scuba holidays are a perennial source of enjoyment for untold numbers of visitors. Diving is regulated by the government to international certification standards, which means that a medical check is an essential prerequisite if you want to dive seriously around Malta. Department of Health inspectors regularly inspect the compressors at diving schools. There is a recompression chamber/hyperbaric unit at St Luke's Hospital (tel: 2123 4765/6 or 196).

The waters around Malta and Gozo are virtually tideless and underwater currents in summer are rare. Moreover, due to the short distances involved, divers can easily change dive localities at short notice. As speedboat and other surface traffic is heavy, it is mandatory to fly the code-A flag or use surface marker buoys.

The following are the most popular in a wide range of Maltese diving sites:
- Delimara Point
- Wied iz-Zurrieq
- Ghar Lapsi
- Anchor Bay
- Cirkewwa
- Ahrax Point
- Qawra Point
- Merkanti Point

Gozo sites at Dwejra, Reqqa Point, Xlendi and Marsalforn are popular, as is Comino.

In Malta, diving schools are mainly located in Mellieha, Sliema-St Julian's, Bugibba-Qawra and Marsascala.

In Gozo there are schools at Xlendi and Marsalforn, and there is one on Comino. Most schools teach courses for beginners that start in shallow hotel pools, as well as

Right: ready to plumb the depths of the Blue Lagoon

advanced PADI/CMAS two-star divers courses. Most schools offer wetsuits and all the necessary equipment. All authorised diving parties are accompanied by an experienced guide – who must be a fully qualified diving instructor.

Major hotels that run their own schools include the following:
- Suncrest Hotel, Qawra; tel: 2157 7101
- Dolmen Resort Hotel, Bugibba; tel: 2158 1510
- Seabank Hotel, Mellieha; tel: 2157 3116
- Paradise Bay Hotel, Cirkewwa; tel: 2157 3981

Other schools include the following:
- Sport Diving, Marsascala ; tel: 2182 9418
- Divecare, St. Julian's; tel: 319994
- Scubatech Diving Centre, Rabat; tel. 2145 5916
- St Andrew's Divers' Cove, Xlendi, Gozo; tel: 2155 1301
- Comino Beach Centre, Comino; tel: 2152 9821

Sailing

The Royal Malta Yacht Club (Manoel Island, tel: 2133 3109) is a focal point for sailing. The club is situated in Marsamxett and has a splendid view across the water to the Valletta bastions. The main annual event is the Middle Sea Race in July. Sailing schools around the islands that hold competitions include the following:

- Reef Club at St Julian's (tel: 2138 1000)
- Charles Vella Boatyard at Haywharf, Floriana (tel: 2123 6911)
- The Comino Hotel on Comino island (tel: 2152 9821), which offers good facilities and splendid sailing around the island's coves. Look out for the hotel's dinghy events, which are particularly popular.

Water-skiing, windsurfing and other water sports

Canoes, paddle boats, jet skis, 'sausage' rides, parakiting, speedboats, water-skiing and windsurfing are all available at the major bays and beaches on both Malta and Gozo throughout the summer and also in winter, when the weather allows.

Many water-sport facilities can be found on site in bays and on the beaches, so look out for the little kiosks that are covered with relevant advertisements. The Borg Ski School (tel: 2157 3272) at Golden Bay hires out water-sport equipment, as do the NSTS Beach Club (tel: 2134 2178) at Qui-Si-Sana, Sliema, and Sun 'n' Fun (tel: 2137 3822) in St George's Bay. Charges are reasonable, but check them out first.

Water polo, which has become quite a popular sport with the Maltese, is played at the National Swimming Pool (tel: 2132 3520) at Tal Qroqq. Major clubs – such as the Sliema Aquatic Sports Club, Neptunes in Balluta Bay, and Sirens (St Paul's Bay) – offer swimming facilities and also feature comprehensive catering facilities for lunches and dinners. Naturally enough, they are all situated in seafront localities.

Horse-racing and riding

The Marsa region has always been associated with horses, whether for riding or racing. The area was popularised by British army and naval officers who utilised the stables for their polo ponies. Today, horse-racing is the island's most popular spectator sport, though trotting, as it is known, bears little resemblance to the thoroughbred affairs familiar to Aintree or Kentucky racegoers. The Malta Racing Club (tel: 2122 4800) organises a busy calendar of races through most of the year.

If you would rather ride than watch races, there are a number of schools, mainly in the Marsa area, including Star Horse Riding (tel: 9985 7491) and Darmanin's Riding School (tel: 2123 8507). In Gozo, there is Wagon Wheel in Victoria (tel: 2155 6254).

Football

Maltese men are crazy about football. Many of them live, breathe, talk and eat football amid great national and international rivalry. The Malta Football Association (tel: 2123 2581/2122 6897), founded in 1900, is one of the oldest outside Britain. Football is taught at specialised 'nursery' schools, which welcome visitors. Most have a bar and refreshment area. The Malta Football Association's Ta'Qali Technical Complex (tel: 2141 1505) features splendid training facilities, including grass pitches, a fully fitted gymnasium, sauna, conference rooms and physiotherapy centre for sports injuries, all of which are available for hire, as indeed are a number of 5-a-side pitches elsewhere.

sports

Golf

The Royal Malta Golf Club (tel: 2123 3851) at Marsa has, since 1988, endeavoured to meet international standards. The course was laid out by British consultants and now has some 50 sand bunkers designed by David Llewellyn. The locals are particularly fond of golf and it is hoped that enough land will be found somewhere on Malta's tiny islands to make a second golf course.

Keep-fit, jogging and cycling

All major hotels have a gymnasium and keep-fit facilities, most of which are also made available to non-residents. Additionally, most major hotels and resorts have tennis, squash and badminton courts. Large gyms and keep-fit centres outside of hotel premises include the Cynergi Fitness Centre (tel: 2134 1191) at St Julian's, and the Football Association gymnasium (tel: 2143 7023) at Ta'Qali.

Jogging is popular in the early morning. Most joggers pound the wide pavements at Ghar id-Dud, or the Bugibba promenade.

Bicycles and protective helmets can be hired, but be careful of erratic traffic. The best traffic-free run is in central Ta'Qali. For further information, contact the national cycling association (tel: 2143 2954).

Other sports

The main associations of other sports in Malta are as follows:

- Amateur Athletics (tel: 2143 2402)
- Basketball (tel: 2143 0950)
- Billiards/Snooker (tel: 2145 1860)
- Bridge (tel: 2131 2895)
- Darts (tel: 2123 5311)
- Drag Racing (tel: 2146 4591)
- Judo (tel: 2138 1136)
- Karate (tel: 2123 2455)
- Malta Olympic Committee (tel: 2124 1382)
- Table Tennis (tel: 2124 8635)
- Volleyball (tel: 2132 3520).

The Malta Union Club (tel: 2133 2011) and, especially for rugby and cricket, Marsa Sports Club (tel: 2122 7113) are private sports and leisure clubs that welcome non-member visitors.

The Eden Super Bowl (tel: 2138 7398) in St Julian's has 20 bowling lanes, a giant video wall, and internet café facilities.

For children

Major hotels and leisure complexes have 'animation' teams that organise games and activities for children. Malta's Carnival is a major attraction for adults and youngsters. Unlike other European carnivals that have adopted modern themes, Malta's carnival is still a traditional family affair, in which thousands participate on floats and in dance teams. Fiestas are also family affairs but the fireworks are loud, and indulgence in alcohol is an integral part of band marches.

The Popeye Film Set and Village (tel: 2157 2430, on the way to Cirkewwa – bus 441 from Ghadira Bay every hour) is an evergreen popular with children of all ages. Here you can see the set used in the Robin Williams movie after which it was named.

The Playmobil Funpak Centre (Bulebel Industrial Estate, tel: 2169 9045/6; bus 29 from Valletta) stages parties and workshops

that teach assorted crafts. Look out for the special offers on manufactured items.

Check with the tourism authority (tel: 2122 3595) for the schedule of the In Guardia parades. These costumed theme parades depict aspects of Malta's history, much of it connected with the Knights of St John.

The Splash 'N Fun Park (tel: 2137 4283) at Bahar ic-Caghaq has water chutes, children's pools and a model dinosaur park.

The Imax Cinema (tel: 2134 6401) in St Julian's offers wondrous three-dimensional images on a six-storey screen. But don't expect Hollywood blockbusters: the Imax Cinema specialises in documentary and educational films.

Left: windsurfing is one of the most popular local water sports
Right: toddlers in the swim

EATING OUT

Malta's restaurants used to suffer from a terrible reputation, which was not wholly unwarranted. In recent years, however, increasing wealth has broadened and enriched local lifestyles, much as it has throughout the Western world. By the same token, tourism to the islands has increased, which in turn has encouraged the advent of new cafés and restaurants that cater to the sophisticated needs of discriminating visitors and locals alike.

There are not many dishes that might be termed authentically Maltese. For the most part, local cuisine consists of a mixture of Maltese and Italian fare with various other continental influences thrown into the pot. Although a variety of fish are in abundant supply in the waters off the islands, their presence on restaurant menus is always subject to the seasons and the prevailing weather conditions.

Rabbit *(fenek)* is such a popular local dish that many farmers on the islands specialise in breeding rabbits for restaurants. Other local specialities include the following:

Gbejna – a very popular local cheese made from ewe's milk.

Minestra – thick vegetable soup similar to minestrone; another variation, *kawlata*, is made with beans and pork.

Timpana – a baked dish featuring a mixture of ricotta cheese, macaroni/rice, minced meat, tomato purée, aubergines, onions or eggs, all encased in pastry.

Torta tal-Lampuka – a Mediterranean fish dish with tomatoes, cauliflower, onions and olives, all covered with pastry and baked.

Bragjoli – a mixture of meat (usually beef), eggs, onions and breadcrumbs, all wrapped in thin slices of steak before being deep-fried.

Pastizzi – a savoury pastry stuffed with a variety of fillings, such as ricotta cheese, peas or meat, then baked in special ovens and served hot.

Mqaret – diamond-shaped pastry cases filled with a delicious date-based mixture then deep-fried.

Qaghaq tal-ghasel – a ring of pastry filled with treacle and spices.

Drinks

In recent years there has been a great improvement in the quality of Maltese and Gozitan wines. The brands to look for are Meridiana, Marsovin, Camilleri and Delicata.

When it comes to beer, the local brews – Farson's Strong Ale, Blue Label Ale, Cisk Lager and Shandy – are all excellent. Indeed, some argue that they match imported lagers and beers in quality.

Two local drinks might stimulate your curiosity. The label on Farson's Lacto Milk-Stout states: 'with Vitamin B for extra strength'. By contrast, Kinnie, a somewhat bitter fizzy drink, is something of a local

Above: there is no shortage of tranquil options when it comes to eating out

eating out

answer to Coca-Cola or root beer. Both are acquired tastes but worth trying.

The majority of bars and cafés are open 9am–1am. There are no age restrictions on the consumption of alcohol.

All restaurant bills include government tax. Some restaurants have recently started to follow the European custom of adding a service charge to the bill – usually between 10 and 12 percent. If the service charge is not included, its payment is at your discretion.

The following list of restaurants and cafés, all of which are recommended, are in geographical order. Unless noted, they all take major credit cards. Advance booking at most is necessary, especially at weekends and in the summer.

The following ratings are based on an average meal for two:

$ Lm10–15
$$ Lm15–20
$$$ Lm20–25

Malta

Valletta

Ambrosia
Archbishop Street
Tel: 2122 5923
Charming, fashionable, quiet atmosphere, good food. Booking essential. $$$

Blue Room
59 Republic Street
Tel: 2123 8014
Chinese cooking highly regarded by locals. Booking recommended. $$

Caffè Cordina
244 Republic Street
Tel: 2123 4385
www.caffecordina.com
A Maltese institution known to locals as the 'Italian café', try the *ricotta pastizzi* (hot, savoury pastries) and wonderful cappuccino. It also sells traditional seasonal confections, such as *Figolas* at Easter. $

The Carriage
Valletta Buildings
South Street
Tel: 2124 7828
Imaginative cuisine at an elegant restaurant on the top floor of an office block, with won-

derful views. Lunch Mon–Fri, dinner Fri and Sat. Booking essential. $$$

La Cave
Castille Square
Tel: 2124 3677
Pastas, pizzas and salads at a friendly wine bar underneath the Hotel Castille. La Cave benefits from the adjoining hotel's extensive wine list. $–$$

Da Pippo Trattoria
136 Melita Street
Tel: 2124 8029
A small, unpretentious restaurant with green painted tables and chairs that is popular with locals and visitors alike. Simple, delicious, well-prepared dishes. Often crowded, so reserve a table. $$

Giannini
St Michael's Bastion (off Windmill Street)
Tel: 2123 7121; fax: 2123 6875
e-mail: giannini@maltanet.net
One of Valletta's highly regarded restaurants, on account of food that never fails to please, wonderful views and pleasant ambience. The bar is located on the ground floor of a patrician house – take the lift up two flights to the dining rooms, which overlook Marsamxett Harbour with Manoel Island and Sliema across the water. When the weather is warm and sunny, try to secure one of the five balcony tables. Giannini serves lunch every day, except Sun, dinner on Fri and Sat only. $$$

Malata
Palace Square
Tel: 2123 3967
One of Valletta's oldest restaurants, Malata was recently taken over by new management but still specialises in both Maltese

Right: Bologna, for a taste of Italy

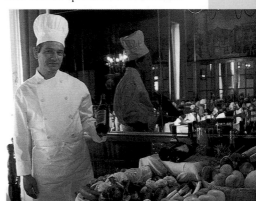

Portopalo Restaurant
30 Tigne Sea Front
Tel: 2133 1915
The decor is simple, but the cuisine is well prepared. When ordering fish be sure to ascertain the price beforehand. $$–$$$

Vino Veritas
59 Dingli Street
Tel: 2132 4273
Inexpensive dishes, so always crowded with young set. Good pasta and daily specials. $$

St Julian's and Paceville
Bouzouki
Spinola Road
Tel: 2131 7127
A long-established Greek restaurant that offers friendly service and wonderful cuisine (the lamb dishes are especially delicious). Relaxed atmosphere. Very little parking. $$

La Dolce Vita
155 St George's Road
Tel: 2133 7036
A restaurant popular with the young and trendy; try for a rooftop table in summer. The trattoria-style food is very good. $$$

Peppino's
31 St George Road
Tel: 2137 3200
Peppino's, which opened in 1991, features a wine bar on the ground floor and restaurants on the two floors above. From the second floor there is access to the terrace – and wonderful views over the bay. Interesting menu. $$–$$$

San Giuliano
Spinola Road
Tel: 2133 2000
A glass-walled affair that overlooks Spinola Bay, San Giuliano is an up-market haunt where people go to be seen. The quality of the food is decidedly uneven. $$$

Terrazza
Spinola Bay
Tel: 2138 4939
Terraced restaurant on the waterfront. Perfect location in summer when fish is a speciality. In winter it turns into indoor trattoria. Booking required. $$$

specialities and Italian cuisine. Benefits from a good location in a vaulted cellar under Palace Square. $$–$$$

Rubino
53 Old Bakery Street
Tel: 2122 4656
Welcoming, fashionable and popular restaurant. Authentic Maltese and Mediterranean dishes. Lunch Mon–Sat. Tues and Fri dinner. Booking essential. $$

Sicilia Bar
14 St John Street/Battery Street
Tel: 2124 0569
A small restaurant with a long family tradition. Delicious Sicilian cuisine and friendly service. There's limited space inside but you can sit outside, where there are beautiful views over the Grand Harbour. Lunch only. $

Sliema
Il Galeone
35 Tigne Sea Front
Tel: 2131 6420
Popular, casual but small restaurant whose house specialities include *spaghetti all'arabbiata*, pasta served as a starter with a very hot sauce. Booking is recommended. $$–$$$

Ta' Kris
80 Fawwara Lane
Tel: 2133 367
In a quiet alley off Bisazza Street, hidden by shops. Cosy, popular haunt with home cooking. $$

Above: pizza is always popular

Mellieha

The Arches
113 Borg Olivier Street
Tel: 2152 3460
www.thearchesmalta.com
Elegant, spacious restaurant with a large walk-in wine cellar that delights wine buffs. Located centrally near the Chapel of St Mary. Varied international menu. Book ahead. $$$

Giuseppi's
25 St Helen Street
Tel: 2157 4882
Popular and typically Maltese – in both ambience and cuisine – whose menu changes daily according to the availability of products in the local market. $$

St Paul's Bay

Gillieru
Near Bugibba
Tel: 2157 3480
Family-owned for over 75 years, Gillieru features a terrace that overlooks the sea and St Paul's Island. Fish is a speciality. $$–$$$

Ta'Cassia Farmhouse
Qawra Road (up the hill from the JFK Memorial Garden), Qawra
Tel: 2157 1435
A converted farmhouse with rustic decor and, in summer, a disco in the garden. $$

Il-Veccia
St Paul's Street
Tel: 2158 2376
Probably the first restaurant to appear in the St Paul's Bay area, more than 100 years ago. Now under new family management with Italian-style cuisine. $$–$$$

Mdina

Bacchus
Inguanez Street
Tel: 2145 4981
www.bacchus.com.mt
Elegant, expensive, international fare. $$$

Ciapetti
5 St Agatha's Esplanade
Tel: 2145 9987
Good location at Bastion Square. Relaxed atmosphere and fine food. $

Fontanella Tea Gardens
Bastion Street
Tel: 2145 4264
Located on the city walls, with wonderful views over the plateau, the Fontanella offers a large selection of Maltese cakes and savoury snacks. Take-away available. $

Medina Restaurant
7 Holy Cross Street
Tel: 2145 4004
Romantically set in one of Mdina's oldest buildings, the Medina is an excellent choice for a long, lazy lunch or dinner. Step into the cool courtyard and feel as if you have travelled back in time. Wheelchair access. $$$

Stazzjon Restaurant
Mtarfa Road
Tel: 2145 1717
Located underneath the city walls, in Mdina's old railway station. Italian-influenced cuisine in an authentic atmosphere. $$

De Mondion at Xara Palace
St Paul's Square
Tel: 2145 0560
www.xarapalace.com.mt
De Mondion is a roof-top restaurant at the Xara Palace hotel with fine French and Italian cuisine: old-style elegance in a quiet setting. Ground floor trattoria for pizza and pasta. $$

Dingli

Bobbyland Bar & Restaurant
Dingli Cliffs
Tel: 2145 2895
Long-established restaurant in a wonderful setting over the Dingli Cliffs. The cuisine is simple but the service is excellent. Popular with locals for an evening out and with businessmen for lunch. Busy at weekends. $$–$$$

Right: mullet destined for a fish dish

Bahrija
North Country Bar
Bahrija (near Rabat)
Tel: 2145 4340
The place to enjoy rabbit Maltese-style. A bit remote, but signposted from Rabat. The locals provide a great atmosphere at weekends. Simple, delicious food and wine. $

Marsascala
Grabiel
Triq Mifsud Bonnici
Tel: 2168 4194
Delicious fish dishes both local and especially flown in. Always crowded. Book ahead. $$$

La Favorita
Gardiel Street
Tel: 2163 4113
Small family-run restaurant with delicious fish. Meat too. Booking recommended. $$

Marsaxlokk
Hunter's Tower
Triq il Kajjik
Tel: 2165 1792
Popular option; serves Maltese dishes. $$

Gozo
Marsalforn
Auberge Ta'Frenc
Between Victoria and Marsalforn
Tel: 2155 3888
Elegance in a converted farmhouse. Good choice for a special date. Dinner only. $$$

Il-Kartell
Marina Street
Tel: 2155 6918
On the seafront and ideal for summer. Italian-style and Maltese dishes, big on fish. $–$$

Smuggler's Cave
2 Marina Street
Tel: 2155 1005
Maltese and Italian dishes, great pizza. Seafront views; carved into the rocks. $–$$

Gharb
Salvina's
Frenc Ta'L-Gharb Street
Tel: 2155 2505
Attractive decor, excellent service and fine location in a traditional Gozitan farming village. Closed Sun. $$

Victoria
It-Tmum
Europe Street
Tel: 2156 6667
Considered Gozo's finest restaurant and certainly it is the prettiest. Always crowded. Mediterranean cuisine. Book ahead. $$$

Xaghra
Gesther
8th September Avenue
Tel: 2155 6621
The island's best bet for good, old-fashioned home cooking. Lunch only. $

Oleander
Victory Square
Tel: 2155 7230
One of the island's most renowned restaurants, Oleander serves good local dishes, plus wonderful fish and steaks. $$

Xlendi
Paradise
Mount Carmel Street
Tel: 2155 6878
Family eatery. Fine fish, seafood dishes. $

Stone Crab & Ta' Karolina
Marina Street
Tel: 2155 6400
Maltese and Italian fish dishes and excellent pizza and snacks. Book in summer. $–$$

Left: fish dish

CALENDAR OF EVENTS

Carnival

Carnival celebrations start the weekend before Lent, with Valletta staging the biggest parade. Inaugurated by the Knights of St John, the festival originally marked the eve of Lenten fasting.

Easter Week

Holy Week is an inspirational time. After Palm Sunday processions and masses, Malta is quiet until Maundy Thursday, when homes, parish halls and churches often present Last Supper displays, a table as it might have been.

On Good Friday pageants feature participants in hooded robes carrying life-sized statues depicting the Passion of Christ.

Saturday may be a day of mourning but Sunday is a day of joy. In the Three Cities, a statue of Christ is carried through the streets. After mass, there is a traditional roast lamb lunch. Children eat *figola*, a marzipan and pastry concoction decorated with icing sugar.

The Festa

The festa season (May–Sept) celebrates local patron saints or religious events such as the Assumption. Features include streets festooned with colourful decorations, band marches, fireworks, and a solemn Mass.

The best fireworks displays are held in the villages of Qormi, Lija, Zurrieq, Mqabba and Qrendi. The best marches are at Hamrun for San Gaetano, for Our Lady of Graces in Zabbar, and in Valletta for the feast of St Paul's Shipwreck.

Other Events

The 42-km (26-mile) *Marathon* is run in **February**. The race, from Mdina to Sliema, has been an annual affair since 1986.

On **31 March**, *Freedom Day* is celebrated with a parade in Valletta, fireworks, and races between *dghajsa* boats, whose brightly painted designs are said to have originated in Phoenician times.

The *Feast of St Joseph the Worker* is celebrated in Valletta on **May Day**.

The *Feast of St Peter and St Paul* (commonly known as *Mnarja*) is held on **29 June** in Rabat and Buskett Gardens. Proceedings begin with races between animals ridden bareback up Racecourse Street. The party, featuring food, wine, brass bands and singing, continues until the early hours.

The ever-popular *Jazz Festival* is held in **mid-July**.

There is copious drinking at the *Malta Beer Festival*, organised by Farsons, the brewers, at the **end of July**.

The *Malta International Air Rally* attracts reputed international air squadrons such as the Red Arrows in **September**.

The Grand Harbour hosts a *regatta* on **8 September**, Our Lady of Victories Day, to celebrate victories over the Turks in 1565 and the Axis Powers in 1945.

Republic Day on **13 December** is marked by parades, bands and fireworks.

Christmas (**25 December**) is a family affair with gifts exchanged. Manoel Theatre *(see page 89)* stages a classic pantomime written and produced with great enthusiasm and humour.

Above: raising the flag at one of many street celebrations

Practical
Information

GETTING THERE

By Air

Malta International Airport, not far from Gudja in the southeastern part of the island, is a 15-minute drive from Valletta. The bus service from the airport to Valletta is unreliable and not suitable if you have a lot of luggage. A far better option is to take a white taxi – instead of paying at the end of your journey, buy a voucher at the arrivals terminal and present it to the driver.

Air Malta flies to numerous European and North African destinations, and it connects with other European carriers. Flying time from London is just over 3 hours; from Rome, 1½ hours. Many other airlines operate scheduled services to Malta. Charter flights are much cheaper than regular airline flights but are usually only available as part of a package holiday.

By Sea

Car ferries from ports in Italy and Sicily arrive once or twice a week, in both the summer and winter, as part of a service that continues to Tunisia. Drivers can bring a car onto the island without a special permit but should ensure that their insurance is valid in Malta.

The fastest passenger ferry route to Malta is via catamaran from Sicily (but only when the weather allows). Most travel agents can book catamaran tickets for you on request. Otherwise contact: Virtu Rapid Ferries, 3 Princess Elizabeth Terrace, Ta'Xbiex (tel: 2131 8854/5/6).

TRAVEL ESSENTIALS

When to Visit

April and May are delightful although the sea is not yet warm enough for swimming. Flowers are in full bloom, temperatures are balmy, and the crowds have not arrived. September and October are also great: although the flowers are not as abundant, the warmth of the sea more than compensates. December is also pleasant; after the short rainy season, daisy bushes and mustard plants form a yellow carpet over much of the island. Try to avoid the peak months of July and August when the islands are overcrowded and the temperature often rises above 40°C (104°F).

Visas and Passports

A passport entitles visitors from the EU lengthy stays but visitors from the Commonwealth, the US, Canada, Libya, Kuwait and Saudi Arabia may only stay for up to three months. If you want to stay longer, contact Immigration Police, Calcedonius Street, Floriana (tel: 2122 4002). Many other nationals require visas before arriving.

Vaccinations

No inoculations are required for visitors from Europe, the US, Canada and Australia.

Animal Quarantine

Malta, which is free from rabies, imposes a quarantine on all imported animals, unless they are arriving from an EU country with a Pet Passport. If you want to bring a pet, contact the Director of Agriculture, Department of Agriculture, 14 Mikiel Anton Vassallo Street, Valletta, Malta (tel: 21224941).

Left: fishing boats come in many colours
Right: a bus with character

Customs

Visitors from the EU enter through the Green Channel, usually unchecked. Other nationals should check out entitlements before travelling.

Weather

From late April until October, the average daytime temperature is a warm 25°C (75°F). In this summer period the temperature at night rarely falls below 13°C (56°F). This time of year is also Malta's sunniest period, with an average of 10 hours of sunshine a day. In July and August temperatures can reach a thermometer-busting 42°C (107°F).

Even in the winter months Malta never suffers from snow and frost, but it can be rainy, and the winds can be harsh, especially in January and February. The rainy season falls between November and March.

Clothing

In summer, you don't need to bring anything more than loose cotton clothing; but you should avoid synthetics. Sunglasses and a hat with a brim are essential protection against the sun. An extra layer is useful for the cooler evenings. Between October and May, bring a waterproof jacket or umbrella; in winter months, add a heavy sweater and strong shoes.

Men will require a jacket for some of the more formal restaurants.

Electricity

The current is 220/240-volt and 110 for shavers; some electrical outlets require the British three-prong, flat-pin plug; others have the round, European, two-prong plug.

Time Zones

Malta is in the Central Europe time zone (one hour ahead of GMT). In the period between 31 March and the last Sunday in October, clocks are set another hour ahead.

GETTING ACQUAINTED

Geography

The Republic of Malta, located in the centre of the Mediterranean Sea, consists of three inhabited islands, of which Malta itself is the largest. A land of terraced hills and rocky coasts, Malta has no rivers and few trees. Gozo is situated to the northwest and has much lusher vegetation. Comino lies between Malta and Gozo.

Government and Economy

In September 1964, after years of protection by other countries, the Maltese islands finally became an independent state with a parliamentary democracy. In May 2004 it became an EU member. Today, tourism accounts for over one-fifth of the country's gross national product. Manufacturing industries, financial services, small businesses and agriculture make up much of the rest.

Religion

Ninety-eight percent of the population of Malta have been baptised into the Roman Catholic faith. The 364 churches on Malta and Gozo constitute the hub of village life. Women should not wear bikini or halter tops when visiting churches and men should wear shirts with sleeves. Very short shorts are inappropriate. Topless and naturist bathing is against the law and punishable by fines.

Catholic

English-language Mass is held at:
• St Dominic, St Dominic's Square, Rabat
• St Paul's Bay Parish Church, St Paul's Street, St Paul's Bay
• St Patrick's, St John's Bosco Street, Sliema
• St Barbara's, Republic Street, Valletta (which also conducts Mass in French and German.)

If you are interested in attending an Italian-language Mass, try St Catherine of Italy, Victory Square, Valletta.

Above: a meeting of like minds

Other Christian
• St Paul's Anglican Cathedral,
West Street, Valletta, tel: 2122 4714
• Holy Trinity Anglican Church, Rudolph
Street, Sliema, tel: 2133 0575
• Union Church of Scotland and Methodist
St Andrews, South Street, Valletta, tel: 2122
2643
• Greek Orthodox Church, 83 Merchants'
Street, Valletta, tel: 2122 1600

Other Denominations
• Jewish Community Secretary, Spur Street,
Valletta, tel: 2162 5717
• Islamic Mosque, Kordin, Paola, tel: 2169
7203

Population and Language
Malta has been deeply influenced by all of
the assorted cultures that, at some point in its
history, dominated the islands. Architecture
and cuisine in particular are a mixture of
north African and southern European. As a
result of the islands' eclectic range of genetic
legacies, a *mañana* mentality coexists with
a healthy regard for the work ethic.

The Malti language has an Arabic base
but is written in the Latin alphabet. English,
the second language, is spoken well by the
vast majority of Maltese people. Italian is
also widely spoken.

MONEY MATTERS

Currency
The Maltese lira (Lm) is sometimes known
as the Maltese pound. The lira is divided
into 100 cents. There are Lm2, Lm5, Lm10,
Lm20 and Lm50 notes; 1c, 2c, 5c, 10c, 25c,
50c and Lm1 coins.

Credit Cards
Major credit cards are accepted virtually
everywhere, even at village street markets.
Visa and Mastercard logos are seen most
often, American Express less so.

The American Express Card office is at
14 Zachary Street, Valletta (tel: 2123 2141).

Tipping
The Maltese generally expect to be tipped.
Some restaurants now include a service

charge of 10–12 percent. In most cases
tipping is at the diner's discretion; 10 percent
is adequate. For airport porterage, 50c; for
a hotel chambermaid, Lm1 (per week). Don't
feel obliged to tip taxi drivers, especially if
the service is less than satisfactory.

Changing Money
When it comes to changing money, you may
have to pay a small commission, and rates
vary. The Bank of Valletta and HSBC give
competitive rates. Bring your passport for
identification. Hotels may give a poorer rate
of exchange but accept travellers' cheques;
shops and restaurants will take only cash
(Maltese and British sterling) or credit cards.

You are not allowed to import more than
Lm50; Lm25 is the maximum you can take
out. Keep all exchange receipts, which you
will need when converting Maltese money
into foreign currency.

Banking Hours
1 Oct–14 June: Mon–Fri 8.30am–12.30pm,
(plus Fri 4.30–6pm), Sat 8.30am–noon. 15
June–30 Sept: Mon–Fri 8am–noon (plus Fri
2.30–4pm), Sat 8am–11.30am.

If the banks are closed, you can take
advantage of a 24-hour, 365-days-a-year service at the bank at Malta International Airport, and there are ATM card cash machines
in all Bank of Valletta and HSBC branches
and tourist resorts.

Any of the tourist information centres that
are scattered throughout the islands should
be able to supply you with a pamphlet that
lists the opening hours of all bank branches.

Right: capital bank

GETTING AROUND

The Maltese are notoriously erratic drivers. They rarely indicate when turning, will overtake on the inside and reverse into main roads. Traffic regulations and traffic lights are routinely ignored. For what it's worth, the official speed limits are: 64kph (40mph) on motorways and 40kph (25mph) in urban areas. Although, like the British, the Maltese drive on the left-hand side, the mentality on the roads is decidedly Mediterranean in character.

Parking is another potential cause of headaches. It can be difficult to find a space, and if you park illegally, police and traffic wardens will be quick to pounce.

These problems notwithstanding, it is worth renting a car in Malta (although you ought to take at least one fun ride on the old, rambling buses that run frequently all over the island). Obviously, driving affords you a freedom that public transport does not, and the taxi option works out very expensive after a couple of rides. If you do rent a car, drive defensively, go with the flow and, above all, don't try to beat the locals at their own crazy game.

To hire a car you need only your national driving licence. Petrol prices in Malta are comparable to those elsewhere in Europe, but at least most types of hired car are economical. Petrol stations are generally open 7am–6pm, but have self-service machine facilities after hours.

Car Hire

Most major international car hire firms have outlets here; in summer, you should book ahead. You must be 25 years old (or 21, with fully comprehensive insurance), and produce a driving licence or an international driver's permit. Many car rental firms also offer a selection of chauffeur-driven cars. To hire a car in Malta, try any of the following companies:

John's Garage
38 Villambrosa Street, Hamrun
Tel: 2123 8745

Avis Rent-a-Car
59 Msida Seafront
Tel: 2123 5751

Wembley's Rent-a-Car
50 St George's Road, St Julian's
Tel: 2137 4141/4242
St Andrew's Road, St Andrew's
Tel: 2138 9871

Gozo United Rent-a-Car
5 Xaghra Road, Victoria
Tel: 2155 6144

Taxis

Taxis (usually white Mercedes) can be found at taxi ranks, the airport, harbours and hotels. Ask the driver to run the meter or agree on a fare. On arrival at the airport you can pre-pay an official fare.

Above: travel at your preferred pace

Buses

The public bus system, on which many local people depend, is both reliable and inexpensive. In Malta, most bus routes terminate at the main station just outside the city gates of Valletta. Fares, which are charged according to zones, will never set you back more than 60 cents.

Bus services commence at about 5.30am and finish at around 10pm on weekdays and 11pm on weekends. Free Route maps are available at bus terminals and tourist offices. For details in Malta, tel: 2123 1216. In Gozo, where services are less frequent, the main terminal (tel: 2155 9344) is on Triq Putirjal in Victoria.

Water Transport

A car and passenger ferry operates between Cirkewwa in Malta and Mgarr Harbour in Gozo, from 5.30am (7am from Cirkewwa) with up to 21 crossings daily; travel time is about 25 minutes. In summer, ferry services continue into the night. A non-stop shuttle service also operates during peak holiday periods.

For details contact the Gozo Channel Co, at Mgarr (tel: 2155 6114 or 2156 1622); for Cirkewwa, tel: 2158 0435 or 2157 1884.

To get to Comino, the Comino Hotel runs a ferry service to Cirkewwa. Contact the Comino Hotel (tel: 2152 9821) for details.

A daytime passenger ferry operates across Marsamxett between The Strand in Sliema and the foot of St Mark's Street in Valletta (Apr–Nov). Crossing time is ten minutes.

Helicopter

A helicopter service makes up to nine flights a day in summer to the airfield by the Gozo Experience. Contact Malta Airport (tel: 2122 9990) or Gozo Heliport (tel: 2156 1301).

Bicycles and Motorcycles

Cyclists, motorcyclists and passengers are obliged to wear a helmet. Only the bravest of cyclists venture into the streets of the cities. Try any of the hire shops listed below, of which only the last two rent bicycles:

La Ronde
10 Triq Belvedere, Gzira
Tel: 2132 2962

Right: ideal for narrow roads

Pedal Power
Valletta Road, Mosta
Tel: 2141 6963

Albert's Scooter Shop
200 Triq San Albert, Gzira
Tel: 2134 0149
Also a branch in Bugibba. Tel: 2158 3308

Victoria Cycles Shop
Triq Fortunato Mizzi, Victoria, Gozo
Tel: 2155 3741

Cycle Store
135 Eucharistic Congress Street, Mosta
Tel: 2143 2890
Bicycles only.

Carriages

Karozzin horse-drawn carriages were once Malta's primary mode of transport, but today they are more of a tourist attraction. Prices vary but are generally about Lm5–Lm10 for half an hour for two people. Make sure you agree on the fare before setting out.

A jaunt in a *gharry* (a light horse-drawn carriage) is a picturesque way to take in the sights of Valletta, St Julian's, Sliema and Mdina. The driver should double as a guide, and will doubtless provide you with a photo-opportunity at the reins.

On Foot

Malta and Gozo are great places for walkers. *Landscapes of Malta* (Sunflower Books) is an excellent guide for walking tours but check that you have an up-to-date edition.

Maps

The map that accompanies this book plots all the routes described. It is also useful for independent excursions of your own.

Other good maps include *Bartholomew Clyde Leisure Map of Malta and Gozo* (which highlightss bus routes), *The A to Z Guide to the Streets of Malta* by A Attard Francis, the *Tourist Atlas of the Maltese Islands*, and the 1:25,000 map series *(West Malta; East Malta; Gozo/Comino)* published by the Works Department.

HOURS & HOLIDAYS

Business Hours

Malta takes a siesta 12.30–3.30pm (to 4 or 4.30pm in summer). Businesses generally open 8.30am–5pm; in summer government and some other offices open 7am–1pm. Shops usually open 9.30am–12.30pm and 3– 7 or 8pm (from 4pm in summer). Official museum opening hours: Malta daily 9am–5pm; Gozo Mon–Sat 8.30am–4.30pm, Sun till 3pm.

Public Holidays

New Year's Day	1 January
St Paul's Day	10 February
St Joseph's Day	19 March
Freedom Day	31 March
Good Friday	variable
St Joseph's Day	1 May
'Sette Giugno'	7 June
SS Peter and Paul	29 June
Assumption	15 August
Victory Day	8 September
Independence Day	21 September
Feast of the Immaculate Conception	8 December
Republic Day	13 December
Christmas Day	25 December

ACCOMMODATION

Hotels are rated according to international standards with one- to five-star status. There are also aparthotels and a number of licensed guest-houses. Prices correspond roughly with their star rating (based on a double-room with private facilities):

Five-star Lm 70–140
Four-star Lm 40–70
Three-star Lm 30–45
Two star Lm 20–30. Check if there are private facilities.
One star under Lm 20. Check if there are private facilities.

Malta

Castille***
348 Triq San Pawl
Valletta
Tel: 2124 3677
www.hotelcastillemalta.com
Within the city walls across the street from the Auberge de Castille, the Castille features splendid views across the Grand Harbour and Valletta.

Le Meridien Phoenicia*****
The Mall
Floriana
Tel: 2122 5241
e-mail: info@phoenicia.com.mt
One of the island's first hotels, dating back to a time when mass tourism was unknown. Set in a gorgeous colonial-style building situated just outside Valletta. Its numerous amenities include conference facilities.

Kennedy Nova****
116 Triq ix-Xatt
Sliema
Tel: 2134 5480
e-mail: info@kennedynova.com.mt
Situated in the outskirts of Sliema and right on the seafront, the Kennedy Nova has benefited from an ambitious expansion programme that has boosted its popularity.

Fortina Spa Resort****
Tigne Sea Front
Sliema
Tel: 2346 0000
www.hotelfortina.com

Left: a ferry arrives

Well-situated near Sliema's shopping centre, the Fortina's waterfront location offers fine views across Marsamxett harbour and Valletta. Excellent spa and health facilities. The Fortina has seven restaurants including Japanese and Indian.

Intercontinental*****
St George's Bay
St Julian's
Tel: 2137 7600
www.malta.intercontinental.com
In entertainment district with rooftop pool and beach lido.

Marina***
Tigne Sea Front
Sliema
Tel: 2133 6461
www.themarinahotelsliema.com
The Marina is within walking distance of the Sliema bus terminus and The Strand, which is the departure point for most sea excursions. The views across the creek to Valletta are a definite plus.

Crowne Plaza Hotel*****
Tigne Street
Sliema
Tel: 2134 1173
www.crowneplaza.com/malta
A holding of Air Malta, and formerly a Holiday Inn, the Crowne Plaza benefits from a tasteful conversion of late 19th- and 20th-century buildings. Though most popular as a conference centre, it is also well endowed with leisure activities. Situated in a quiet area that is convenient for Sliema and not far from St Julian's.

Preluna****
124 Tower Road
Sliema
Tel: 2133 4001
www.preluna-hotel.com
Situated at the Ghar id-Dud focal point on the Sliema seafront, the Preluna is surrounded by restaurants and coffee shops in the midst of Sliema's commercial district.

Park Hotel****
Graham Street
Sliema
Tel: 2134 3780
www.parkhotel.com.mt
Situated just off the popular Tower Road. The Park Hotel has a good leisure centre with indoor pool, restaurant and roof pool with great view.

Howard Johnson Diplomat****
173 Tower Road
Sliema
Tel: 2134 5361
www.diplomat.com.mt
Reasonable rates, the Diplomat hotel is both practical and comfortable. Rooftop pool and good restaurants.

Europa**
138 Tower Road
Sliema
Tel: 2133 0080
www.europahotel-malta.com
Conveniently situated between Sliema and St Julian's. Small and compact.

Astoria*
46 Point Street
Sliema
Tel: 2133 2089
Small hotel opposite It-Torri, a landmark tower after which Tower Road is named.

Golden Tulip Vivaldi****
Dragonara Road
St Julian's
Tel: 2137 8100
www.goldentulipvivaldi.com
Slap-bang in the centre of Paceville, the Golden Tulip Vivaldi is comfortable, well-furnished, and surrounded by scores of restaurants and bars.

Above: poolside and seaside at Le Meridien Phoenicia

Westin Dragonara Resort***
Dragonara Road
St Julian's
Tel: 2138 1000
www.westinmalta.com
One of the generation of new five-star hotels clustered around Paceville. Superb location and sea views. Excellent conference and leisure facilities, complete with Reef Club. Near the casino at Dragonara.

Hilton***
Portomaso
St Julian's
Tel: 2133 6201
www.malta.hilton.com
Part of a Portomaso business and leisure complex complete with office tower, yacht marina and private apartments.

Radisson SAS Baypoint***
St George's Bay
St Julian's
Tel: 2137 4894
www.islandhotels.com
A recent addition with top conference and leisure facilities, overlooking busy St George's Bay and with good proximity to Paceville's throbbing nightlife.

Corinthia San Gorg***
St George's Bay
St Julian's
Tel: 2137 4114
www.corinthiahotels.com
One of a chain of Maltese and international hotels owned by the Corinthia Group, Malta's largest leisure concern. Conference and leisure oriented.

Forum**
St Andrew's Road
St Andrew's

Tel: 2137 0324
Situated between St Julian's and St Paul's Bay, the Forum enjoys a quiet location and offers reasonable rates.

Coastline**
Salina Bay
Salina
Tel: 2157 3781
www.islandhotels.com
Situated in a quiet spot on the road leading to Qawra, the well-maintained Coastline offers good sea views.

Gillieru Harbour**
Church Square
St Paul's Bay
Tel: 2157 2720
A pleasant, 50-room establishment with good restaurant facilities, the Gillieru also has its own diving school.

Bugibba Holiday Complex**
Triq it-Turisti
Qawra
Tel: 2158 0861
www.islandhotels.com
This is one of the largest holiday complexes in Malta and is generally very popular with visitors on account of its attractive range of rates and central position.

Dolmen Resort Hotel**
Qawra
Tel: 2355 2355
www.dolmen.com.mt
The New Dolmen features its own diving school, a convention centre and, for those who appreciate an active nightlife, a casino and a new nightclub. The swimming pool compounds and leisure facilities have both been recently upgraded and now feature a spa and indoor pool.

Suncrest**
Qawra Coast Road
Qawra
Tel: 2157 7101
www.suncresthotel.com
This large, 413-room hotel features several restaurants, bars, a disco, 24-hour coffee shop, good pool and leisure areas. Lots of summer entertainment.

Left: relaxing at the Dolmen Resort Hotel

Qawra Palace****
Qawra Coast Road
Qawra
Tel: 2158 0131
www.qawrapalacemalta.com
Together with the Suncrest Hotel, the Qawra Palace constitutes the life and soul of this part of the Qawra seafront.

Santana****
Gozo Road
Qawra
Tel: 2158 3451
e-mail: info@santanahotel.com
A recent addition to the list of hotels in Qawra, the Santana is centrally situated and in walking distance of an abundance of restaurants and bars.

Grand Mercure Selmun Palace****
Selmun
Mellieha
Tel: 2152 1040
One of the most secluded hotels on the island. It is located on a hill centred around the core of the old Selmun Palace and commands wonderful views of the island and across the Gozo Channel.

La Salita****
Main Street
Mellieha
Tel: 2152 0923
www.maritimmalta.com
Originally created as a family enterprise right in the centre of Mellieha, La Salita enjoys a good location that is not too far from Malta's largest sandy beach.

Mellieha Bay****
Ghadira Bay
Tel: 2157 3844
www.melliehabayhotel.com
A forerunner of the Malta holiday boom, the Mellieha Bay established a reputation for package holidays and fun entertainment. Conveniently situated on the Ghadira waterline with splendid views across the island's largest sandy bay.

Ramla Bay Resort****
Ramla Bay
Marfa

Tel: 2152 2183
www.ramlabayresort.com
Recently refurbished hotel situated in a quiet location, and good for leisure and water sports, including sailing.

Paradise Bay*****
Cirkewwa
Tel: 2157 3981
www.paradise-bay.com
On Malta's northern coastal shore and within walking distance of the Gozo ferries.

Corinthia Palace*****
De Paule Avenue
Attard
Tel: 2144 0301
www.corinthiahotels.com
The Corinthia Palace, complete with 158 elegantly furnished rooms, offers all the luxury you would expect of a five-star hotel. The breakfast buffet is magnificent. There is an Athenaeum health and beauty centre in the courtyard, and the oriental restaurant, The Rickshaw, is one of the best in Malta. Situated next to San Anton Gardens in a quiet area well served by a public bus service and the hotel's courtesy buses.

Jerma Palace****
Dawriet it-Torri
Marsascala
Tel: 2163 3222
www.corinthiahotels.com
The only hotel of any size in the south of the island. Situated in a quiet area with a

Right: the luxurious Mercure Selmun Palace

www.grandhotelmalta.com

The Grand is situated up the hill from the Gozo ferry terminal on the road to the small village of Ghajnsielem. Splendid views across the water.

Kempinski Hotel San Lawrenz***
San Lawrenz
Tel: 2155 8640
www.kempinski-gozo.com

Close to the village of San Lawrenz on the road to Dwejra, the San Lawrenz resort is elegantly built into a valley. The rooms are centred around a complex of pools shaded by palm trees. Good restaurant and health spa and extensive parking facilities.

St Patrick's**
Xlendi
Tel: 2156 2951
www.vjborg.com

Recently rebuilt and affording a splendid view over Xlendi Bay, St Patrick's features indoor and outdoor restaurants, and a friendly, family atmosphere.

Atlantis*
Qolla Street
Marsalforn
Tel: 2155 4685
www.atlantisgozo.com

Situated in a quiet area of Marsalforn with good proximity to a fitness centre, Atlantis is also within walking distance of any number of restaurants and bars.

Farm and country houses in Gozo

These cosy, rustic stone dwellings constitute a popular form of holiday accommodation in Gozo. An integral feature of the villages and countryside, they have been converted from either mini-fortresses built hundreds of years ago, or from crumbling old farm houses. Some, built more recently, faithfully copy the farm-house style.

A good option when staying in this type of accommodation is to hire a housekeeper and/or a cook. In a number of areas the houses are grouped together in a complex featuring a communal swimming pool and leisure facilities. Any major travel agency should be able to help you reserve accommodation in one of these places.

waterfront location. Close to restaurants and bars but for touring you will need a car.

Xara Palace***
St Paul's Square
Mdina
Tel: 2145 0560
www.xarapalace.com.mt

In one of Malta's oldest palazzi, with great historic connections, the Xara Palace has been plushly finished. From its roof you can see virtually the whole of Malta on a clear day. There are only 18 rooms available and peace and quiet is guaranteed. There is a rooftop restaurant. A member of the Relais & Châteaux association.

Gozo
Cornucopia**
Gnien Imrik Street
Xaghra
Tel: 2155 6486
www.vjborg.com

The Cornucopia has splendid views across Xaghra Valley and down to Marsalforn Bay, a friendly atmosphere, good Friday evening buffets, and self-catering apartments.

Ta'Cenc***
Sannat
Tel: 2155 6830
www.vjborg.com

A much sought-after hotel that melts into the countryside. The single-storey buildings have luxury rooms. Expensive, exclusive and quiet.

Grand**
St Anthony Street
Ghajnsielem
Tel: 2156 3840

Above: the Cornucopia Hotel also offers self-catering apartments

HEALTH & EMERGENCIES

Health Matters

Most well-known medicines are available in Malta but bring your own if you have a specific problem.

Bring insect repellent creams and sprays; beware of jellyfish which are sometimes found offshore. In some places it is wise to wear rubber or plastic shoes in the sea to protect your feet from sea-urchins.

Tap water is safe to drink, but avoid water from fountains.

Take precautions, even in winter, when out in the sun. Use a high SPF factor suncream or total sun-block for the first few days of your visit, and change to a lower rated suncream when you have acclimatised. You can find most popular brands in shops and pharmacies.

Pharmacies

Pharmacies are not difficult to find as there are many of them in Malta and Gozo. Each one has a green neon cross over its door. Opening hours generally range from 8.30 or 9am until 1pm and 3.30–7pm. Look in *The Times* for a listing of pharmacies open over the weekend.

EU countries, Australia, Tunisia and Turkey have reciprocal health agreements with Malta. Otherwise, make sure you have adequate health insurance. All doctors and dentists on Malta and Gozo speak English and Italian. If you need a doctor, the staff at your hotel should be able to put you in touch with a local one.

Emergency Services

Ambulance/emergency service:
Malta, *tel: 112*
Gozo, *tel: 112*

St Luke's Hospital

Gwardamangia, near Valletta
Tel: 2124 1251/2123 4101
Malta's main hospital.

Craig Hospital

Ghin Qatet Street, Victoria
Tel: 2156 1600
This is the only hospital on Gozo.

Right: for home thoughts

Safety

Malta is still a comparatively safe place for tourists, but it is still necessary to use common sense. This includes not leaving money or valuables on the beach while you swim, and not carrying large amounts of cash. Many hotels offer safety boxes for guests' valuables.

The only known black spot for petty theft is the parking area at Peter's Pool on Delimara Peninsula. In case of theft or attack, notify the police and, if necessary, seek assistance from your embassy. Be sure to obtain documentation supporting your claim, so that you can claim a refund on insurance.

Police

Malta Police Headquarters

Calcedonius St, Floriana
Tel: 2122 4001/2

Gozo Police Headquarters

113 Republic Street, Victoria
Tel: 2156 2046/8

Emergency numbers:

Malta/Gozo, *tel: 112*
Police emergency, *tel: 191*

Illicit Drugs

Don't even think about it. The conservative Maltese impose stiff penalties.

Complaints

The Malta Tourism Authority *(see page 90)* will deal with any serious complaints which you cannot settle personally.

COMMUNICATIONS & NEWS

Postal Services

Post offices in most towns and villages open Mon–Sat 7.45am–1pm. In Valletta and in Victoria on Gozo, the main post offices stay open until 6pm and 5.15pm respectively. You can buy stamps from newsagents, hotels and some souvenir shops. Malta's letter-boxes are red, like British ones.

Postcards or letters to European countries currently cost 16c.

Main Post Office, Malta
Maltapost Head Office
305 Tniq Hal-Qormi, Marsa
Tel: 2122 4422

Maltapost, Gozo
129 Republic Street, Victoria
Tel: 2155 6435

Telephone, Fax, E-mail & Internet

The telephone system has been upgraded to include the Internet, e-mail, etc. It is now possible to dial any country on the international direct dialling system if you know the necessary prefix.

Use call-boxes for local calls; they take phone cards as well as 5c coins. Local and long-distance calls can be made and faxes sent from Maltacom offices at various localities. There are a number of Internet cafés in Sliema, Paceville, Valletta, Bugibba and Qawna, and on Gozo.
International dialling codes:
Denmark: 0045
France: 0033
Germany: 0049
Netherlands: 0031
Norway: 0047
Ireland: 00353
Italy: 0039
Spain: 0034
Sweden: 0046
UK: 0044
USA/Canada: 001

For international directory enquiries, dial 1152. For operator assistance in Malta, dial 194; on Gozo, dial 1182.

Media

The Times, one of Malta's two English-language daily papers, is the best source of information on current events.

Most of the major European daily papers are delivered on the afternoon of publication; periodicals a day later. (On Gozo, the schedule is a day later for both newspapers and periodicals.)

The national broadcasting company of Malta is TVM. It and five independent television stations air local programmes in Maltese and English plus an assortment of American, Australian and British offerings.

Most Italian TV broadcasts also reach the Maltese islands.

Malta has cable TV and most hotels catering to tourists are wired for SkyNews, CNN, and selected British, French and German channels.

Radio Malta 1 (999kHz medium wave) has local news and music. Radio Malta 2 (93.7VHF/FM) plays popular music; both of these stations broadcast in Maltese only. There are about a score of commercial radio stations, none of which currently broadcast in English.

USEFUL INFORMATION

Facilities for the Disabled

Despite efforts by hoteliers and others in the tourist industry, it's still difficult to sightsee in Malta if you're physically disabled. The terrain of the country makes it difficult to navigate a wheelchair.

For information regarding facilities contact: the Health Education Unit, tel: 2122 4071 or the National Commission for the Handicapped, tel: 2148 7789.

Students

NSTS
(Student and Youth Travel Organisation)
220 St Paul's Street, Valletta
Tel: 2124 9983; 2124 6628
and *45 St Francis Square, Victoria, Gozo*
Tel: 2155 3977
www.nsts.org
The booklet *Student Saver Discount Scheme* lists shops, exhibitions, restaurants and transport offering discounts to those with an ISIC (International Student Identity Card).

Children

There are few facilities especially designed for youngsters (Malta and Gozo aren't ideal for children), but Popeye Village *(see page 46)* and Rinella Film Facilities Studios *(page 38)* should keep them amused for a few hours. For the best sandy beaches, base yourself close to Mellieha or Golden Bay. The place with most to offer children is probably White Rocks (Bahar ic-Caghaq, northwest of Sliema), home to the Splash & Fun Waterpark, and Mediterraneo Marine World.

Gay Scene

There are clubs which welcome gays and lesbians, but their popularity changes fairly frequently, so it is best to take advice locally. It is worth checking out the regularly updated Gay Malta Web Site *(www.gaymalta.org)*, for news on clubs, bars and upcoming events.

The age of consent on Malta is 16.

Nude Bathing

Nude bathing for all and topless bathing for women is officially prohibited, though it is practised on some of the more secluded beaches. A fine, jail or deportation can result if you are prosecuted.

The Arts

The theatre season runs from October to May. Many events, including concerts, plays and pantomime (at Christmas), are staged at the Manoel Theatre in Valletta; check *The Times* for a current programme.

Manoel Theatre
Old Theatre Street
Tel: 2124 6389
www.teatrumanoel.com.mt
This is one of the oldest theatres still in use in Europe. Tours of the theatre are available.

St James Cavalier Centre for Creativity
Valletta
Tel: 2123 1914
www.sjcav.org
A new arts centre in a fortification built by the Knights. A theatre-in-the-round, gallery, cinema and café. See newspapers for listings.

Top Left: for keeping in touch
Left: read all about it. **Right:** the interior of the historic Manoel Theatre

practical information

USEFUL ADDRESSES

Malta Tourism Offices Abroad
United Kingdom
Malta Tourism Office
Park House, 14 Northfields,
London SW18 1DD
Tel: 020-8877 6990
Fax: 020-8874 9416

Netherlands
Nationaal Verkeersbureau Malta
Geelvinck Building, 4th Floor,
Singel 540, 1017 AZ, Amsterdam
Tel: 020-20 6207 223

Germany
Fremdenverkehrsamt Malta
Schilerstrasse 30–40, D-60313,
Frankfurt am Main 1
Tel: 069-418 9001

France
Office National du Tourisme de Malte
9 Cité de Trevise,
75009 Paris
Tel: 01 48 00 03 79

Italy
Ente Nazionale per il Turismo di Malta
Via M. Gonzaga 7, 20123 Milano
Tel: 02-8673 3736

United States
Malta National Tourist Office

Empire State Building
New York, NY 100118
Tel: 212-695 9520

Alternatively, a useful website to consult is
www.searchmalta.com, which has all kinds
of information on Malta.

Tourist Offices within Malta
Malta Tourism Authority
Auberge d'Italie
229 Merchants' Street, Valletta
Tel: 2291 5800
Fax: 2191 5893
www.visitmalta.com
email: info@visitmalta.com
This office is not open to personal callers.
For walk-in information, use the following
tourist offices.

Malta
1 City Arcades, City Gate, Valletta
Tel: 2123 7747
Fax: 2125 5844
Arrivals Lounge
Malta International Airport
Tel: 2369 6073/4
Spinola Palace, Spinola Bay, St Julian's
Tel: 2138 1392

Gozo
Independence Square, Victoria
Tel: 2156 1419
Mgarr Harbour, Gozo
Tel: 2155 3343; 2155 8106

Air Malta Offices
Freedom Square, Valletta
Tel: 2124 0686/8
Tower Road, Sliema
Tel: 2133 0275
Enquiries at Malta International Airport:
Tel: 2299 9884
www.airmalta.com

Embassies and Consulates
American Embassy
Development House,
St Anne Street, Floriana
Tel: 2561 4000

Australian High Commission
Ta'Xbiex Terrace, Ta'Xbiex

Above: Popeye Village is popular with children

Tel: 2133 8201/5
Fax: 2134 4059

British High Commission
Whitehall Mansions, Ta'Xbiex
Tel: 2323 0000

French Embassy
130 Melita Street, Valletta
Tel: 2123 3430

German Embassy
Il-Piazzetta, Entrance B,
Tower Road, Sliema SLM 16
Tel: 2133 6531

Italian Embassy
5 Vilhena Street, Floriana
Tel: 2123 3157

Spanish Embassy
32B South Street, Valletta
Tel: 2124 5185

LANGUAGE

Malti, or Maltese, is a Semitic language with roots that go back to Phoenician times. Given that it is both complicated and of no use outside the islands, the Maltese never expect visitors to speak to them in Malti.

English is the second language and is spoken, or at least understood by the vast majority of the population. However, it is pleasing to both parties to be able to return the most basic greetings and phrases in Malti.

Place Names
The following place names are pronounced as follows:
Birzebbuga *beer-tsay-boo-jah*
Dwejra *dway-ruh*
Gharb *ahrb*
Hagar Qim *ajar eem*
Marsaxlokk *marsa-schlock*
Mdina *im-deena*
Mellieha *mell-ee-ah*
Mgarr *im-jar*
Paceville *par-tchay-ville*
Qawra *ow-rah*
Tarxien *tar-shin*
Xaghra *shah-ra*

Xewkija *show-key-yah*
Xlendi *sch-len-dee*

Useful Phrases
Good morning/*Bongu (bon-jew)*
Good evening/*Bonswa (bon-swah)*
Goodbye/*Sahha (sa-ha)*
How are you?/*Kif int?*
I'm very well, thank you/female response: *thaba grazzi (ta-ba gratsee)*, male response: *thajeb grazzi (ta-szeb gratsee)*
Please/*Jekk-joghbok (yeck yogbock)*
Thank you/*Grazzi (grat-see)*
Yes/*Iva (eeva)*
No/*Le (le, with e as in 'get')*

FURTHER READING

History
Abela, A, *Malta: A Panoramic History*
Blouet, B, *The Story of Malta*. London, 1967 (Malta, 1993).
Bradford, Ernle, *The Siege of Malta*. Penguin.
Bridge, Antony, *The Crusades*. Granada.
Hogan, George, *Malta: The Triumphant Years 1940–4*. Robert Hale.

Art and Architecture
Buhagiar, Mario, *Iconography of the Maltese Islands 1400–1900*.
Hughes, Quentin, *The Buildings of Malta 1530–1795*. London, 1967.
Hughes, Quentin, *Malta: A Guide to the Fortifications*. Malta, 1993.
Mahoney, Leonard, *5000 Years of Architecture in Malta*. Malta, 1996.
de Piro, Nicholas, *International Dictionary of Artists Who Painted Malta*.

Others
Apa Publications, *Insight Guide: Malta*. Detailed run-down of the sights, plus background essays, stunning photography and a fact-packed Travel Tips.
Insight Compact Guide: Malta offers the reader an on-the-spot reference guide.
Caruana Galizia, Anne and Helen, *Recipes from Malta*. Progress Press, Malta.
Cassar-Pullicino, Joseph, *Studies in Maltese Folklore*. Malta University Publications.
Eco, Umberto, *Foucault's Pendulum*. Secker & Warburg.

practical information

www.insightguides.com

INSIGHT GUIDES

The World Leader in Visual Travel Guides & Maps

As travellers become ever more discriminating, Insight Guides is using the vast experience gained over three-and-a-half decades of guide-book publishing to create an even wider range of titles to serve them. For those who want the big picture, Insight Guides and Insight City Guides provide comprehensive coverage of a destination. Insight Pocket Guides supply personal recommendations for a short stay. Insight Compact Guides are attractively portable. Insight FlexiMaps are both rugged and easy to use. And specialist titles cover shopping, eating out, and museums and galleries. Wherever you're going, our writers and photographers have already been there – more than once.

ACKNOWLEDGEMENTS

All photography by	**Glyn Genin** *except*
15T	**Camera Press**
14, 15B, 24T, 24B, 25, 26, 27T, 27B, 30B,	**Lyle Lawson**
32, 34, 35, 36T, 41T, 41B, 42T, 47B, 48,	
55T, 62B, 71, 78, 81, 83,86, 88T, 88B, 89	
12, 13B	**Private Archive**
10, 13T,	**Sovereign Order of St John**
11	**Valletta Museum of Archaeology**
Cover	**Glyn Genin**
Back Cover	**Glyn Genin**
Cartography	**Maria Randall**

INDEX